What Is Your Calling?

The Journey to Find Work You Love

MIKE KAVANAGH

MIKEKAV.COM

What Is Your Calling? The Journey to Find Work You Love
MIKEKAV.COM, Paperback Edition

ISBN: 9798651001941

For My Children
May you have the courage to be yourself
and to follow your heart, always.

Table of Contents

A Brief Introduction

I've been told by some that I have some crazy ideas.

For example, I believe that everyone should be able to have their basic survival needs met without having their lives completely ruled by their jobs. Those survival needs include adequate food and clothing, a home of some sort to live in, some way to get from point A to point B in a reasonable amount of time, and access to medical care when needed. And an iPhone. I'm kidding.

Then there are the other basic needs. A person should have an hour of free time every day to devote to their physical health (like exercise or going for a walk), an hour of free time for mental/emotional/spiritual health (like meditation, prayer, contemplation, journaling, counseling, or whatever suits you), and at least an hour a day for fun, relaxation and spending quality time with family or friends.

A job should not stand in the way of these basic needs, it should support the fulfillment of these needs. And in case there was any doubt about it, it's not truly free time if a person is trying to squeeze these activities in with the looming threat of interruption by an urgent call, text, or email from their employer.

Don't think all of these things are basic needs? Yeah, I don't care about health and happiness either.

Lastly, I believe that meaningful work—work that one feels called to do—should be a reality for anyone who feels that they need that in life.

"Whoa, slow down there," I hear some people saying. "Now you've gone way too far. Not everyone gets to do what they want."

I know, I know, I've heard all the pushback. Most of it is silly when you take the time to really listen to it. But we'll come back to that in a bit. What I'd like to know is… why can't people have all of those basic needs met without the majority of us feeling like slaves? Given the incredible wealth and opportunity that exists in this day and age, why do the things I espouse to be basic needs seem to be a pipe dream? Why couldn't the system we live in support that kind of quality of life for many more people than it does? And why is it that, at least in my corner of the world, it seems as though we are moving away from that ideal rather than toward it?

Because the system is b-r-o-k-e-n. Broken like Communism is broken.

No, this is not an anti-capitalism or anti-free-market rant. I support both of those with the requisite adjustments that help ensure things function as well as possible.

But humor me for a moment and let's take a look at public companies in Corporate America as an example. Their goal is to grow, grow, grow, a bit like the cancer that just got cut off of my arm thanks to me being one of the lucky ones who has my basic medical needs met.

That is because public companies are owned by shareholders, most of whom don't work at the company and simply want a place to stick their money and have it grow at a rate that often defies the laws of physics and common sense. So the companies themselves are literally wired to attempt to achieve those magnificent and usually unrealistic feats at almost any price. They become myopic in their short-term focus and make wonky decisions as a result. It isn't their fault per se, it's just that the financial incentives of the decision-makers are lined up to do that very thing.

So the game becomes all about near-term growth and profit in order to serve the hungry ghost shareholders first and foremost. And serving hungry ghost shareholders first means that customers often take the back seat and employees often get stuffed into the trunk.

Enter unspoken mantra:

More with less! Work harder! Be a better cog in the machine! Take this role that might be sucking your soul, but be grateful, because I'm giving you wages and benefits! And frankly, you should consider yourself as one of the lucky ones because look at all those unemployed people out there (who, incidentally, were the ones we fired in the last downturn and never rehired since it was a lot cheaper to have you do their job on top of your own job).

But I must be careful not to imply that we are simply victims of a system. We play our part in feeding this machine knowingly and unknowingly.

To begin with, we generally choose not to challenge the status quo. And of course, we tend to consume, consume, consume. The problem with that is when our wants and desires far exceed our survival needs, our basic health and happiness needs, and our need for meaningful work, we start to make compromises. These compromises ultimately compete with our ability to fulfill our basic health and happiness needs as well as our need for meaningful work.

Soon enough, we find ourselves stuck in the system and feeling like victims. Worse yet, some of us spend our workdays serving that very system (and I regretfully admit I have fit squarely in this round hole much of my life)... helping to reinforce it and make it that much more deeply entrenched in our culture.

Alright enough with the cynical stuff already. Because I have a dream.

I have a dream that one day, ordinary men and women everywhere will wake up, take stock of their lives, their children's lives, and the lives of those around them, and consciously remove the shackles we have put on each other and ourselves.

I have a dream that we will collectively rise up and shed these values of growth-and-profit-at-the-expense-of-basic-human-well-being and that a movement will begin—one in which our neighbors, friends and family will forego the security of unhealthy jobs that don't support their ultimate good—and that commerce will once again be reigned by ordinary people doing business with other good people in their own communities, supporting a fulfilling way of life for all.

I have a dream that our world's large companies will wake up to find that this movement has taken hold, and that they must change the way they think and behave to survive in this new, fulfilling world where people's wellbeing is placed above the values of shareholder returns and consumerism.

I have a dream that companies everywhere will discover their true place in the world—as organizations designed to serve our survival needs, our basic health and happiness needs, and our need for meaningful work—and that this transformation will be driven by bold leaders who choose to take the risk of following that authentic and meaningful path.

I have a dream that people everywhere will begin to wake up and pursue their calling—that freelancers, entrepreneurs, and artists will flourish, and that they will rediscover the simple joy and freedom of following their hearts.

And I have a dream that I am not the only individual who shares in this dream.

If you are somebody who has something more to offer this world and who is willing to take a risk and follow the road less traveled, then take that road my traveling friend. Do it for your own good, but do it for our good as well. Because your inner spark can start a fire around you. We all need your inner spark. The quality of our lives and our children's lives and our children's children's lives depends on it.

PART 1:

What Is Your Calling?

Once upon a time

Once upon a time, I took my first summer job working in a bagel shop. I was sixteen. My first day on the job, a round man with glasses and a mustache walked in the door and ordered a dozen bagels. He spouted out his order in rapid fire and I scrambled to keep up:

"Two Plain, two Pumpernickel, three Cinnamon Raisin, one Asiago Cheese... how many Pumpernickel did you grab? No I said two! And not the Four Cheese one, I said *Asiago* Cheese. And one Pretzel bagel and one Everything bagel... no don't put the Everything bagel in with the rest of them, you're supposed to put it in a separate bag! I'm sorry, am I not being clear enough for you to understand? Do you need me to go slooowwwwwerrrr?"

Sitting at home that evening, I couldn't stop thinking about that interaction. I was rattled. *That pompous guy treated me like I was an idiot before he knew a single thing about me,* I thought to myself. *Is this just how things are when you're working a job serving the general public? If so, count me out. I want nothing to do with it.*

At that moment I made a silent vow that when I reached the end of the summer and finished my time at that job, I would do whatever I had to in life to never have to work a job like that again.

Why am I telling you about my random first job? That'll become clear by the end of my personal story, which I do plan on sharing with you. But we'll get to that a little later.

First, let me dispense with the warnings.

Some of the contents of this book might fuel an already raging fire in certain people, which may or may not be desirable in your particular case. If you're in a delicate headspace working a job you don't like and you're looking for reassurance that things will get better if you just ride it out a little longer, I'll put the fine print in bold:

Set this book down and slowly back away… especially if you're working an office job in Corporate America, a place I spent 15 years of my professional life. No need to be a tough guy/gal about it. Go watch *Office Space* and laugh yourself to sleep. I don't want you throwing up on your shoes and ruining them and then blaming me. Take care of your shoes, please. (Of course if you do press on and you find that you don't even bat an eye at certain parts, you might be the perfect personality type to be a senior executive in Corporate America yourself. Congratulations! You can have my spot.)

Next, let me warn you about my biases, particularly with respect to Corporate America. Here's the quick version:

I seem to have been born with what some have told me are "idealistic tendencies." Specifically, I believe that what we do for our livelihood matters in some way. Meaning, purpose and positive impact are important values to me and I aspire to have plenty of those things when it comes my own livelihood. I'm not comfortable settling when such a huge chunk of my life is spent at work.

But it turns out that most of the job market isn't tailored to meeting the soulful needs of an empathic idealist like me. Indeed, much of the job market is controlled by Corporate America Himself. And if you'll pardon my crassness, He can be a real dick.

In fairness, He isn't a dick to everyone at all times. There are pockets of true goodness, no doubt. That was even true for a portion of my own experience in the 15 years we tangoed together. But my bias wouldn't be there if I didn't think that on the whole, He leaves much to be desired.

I figure he's a He because He still pays men more than women for no real reason and He hasn't figured out that dads deserve meaningful time off to be with their newborn babies because it isn't the 1950s anymore. Much of the time He seems hell-bent on sucking the soul right out of every hopeful idealist and turning each of them into a stable-paycheck-seeking-uber-materialist who forgets that buying more stuff doesn't bring happiness. Then one day that poor soul finds they are hooked on the stable infusion of biweekly cash injections and that they can't seem to escape His clutches regardless of the intensity of pain being inflicted. On the other hand, sufficient time for ourselves does bring more happiness, and for that He has generously offered us a few weeks of paid time off a year, which He has conned us into thinking is reasonable while simultaneously phasing out most of the humane 9-to-5 jobs of yesteryear and making it a requirement for us to stay plugged in all the damn time.

Yeah, I have some opinions.

"But Mike," you ask, "if you're so down on Corporate America, why didn't you just quit instead of doing it for 15 years and being such a whiney baby about it?"

Touché, my friend. Sounds like you have some opinions too.

I was stuck. I didn't have the clarity then that I have now. For much of the time, I was a product of some top-notch brainwashing. I was told from a very young age by my culture what was most important in my "pursuit of happiness," that God-given right my founding fathers went to such great lengths to secure: I needed to go to school, and college, and get a good job, and make good money, and buy a car, and buy a house, and take some vacations, and save for retirement so that I could relax in my old age and eventually go quietly and peacefully in the night.

The problem is I did most of those—save for the fact that I'm a long way from retirement and hopefully not on the verge of going quietly or loudly—and yet I still found myself with a deep sense of lack. As I see it, I was sold one convincing bill of goods that turned out to be w-r-o-n-g. I was conditioned to live according to a set of values that aren't true in my experience, or at the very least they just aren't my values.

Of course I can't blame the brainwashing, since at some point along the way I realized I was trapped in the Matrix and I saw the fallacy in that way of thinking. I recognized that I needed to simply step off the well-worn path of my societal conditioning and take a risk on the road less traveled. But did I do it?

Nope. I stayed stuck. By the time I could see the plight I was in, my patterns of grasping at stability and financial security and my resistance to disrupting my status quo ran so deep in me that I had trouble freeing myself from my self-created shackles. The worthy foes of depression and anxiety weren't enough to get me to change either. Even a profound existential crisis couldn't get me unstuck.

I don't throw any of these terms like "depression" or "existential crisis" around lightly either. My soul was literally being crushed by the grind of my day jobs and it was taking a massive mental, emotional and physical toll on me. I found myself on the edge of an abyss and I truly did fear that I might slip into it and never be able to pull myself out.

Part of what contributed to my feeling so stuck was that my wife and my son depended on me as the sole breadwinner. I didn't want to put them through a ton of disruption unless it was a last resort. Even in the moments when it felt like the time had come to exercise that last resort, I didn't have enough clarity about what I should do next. How could I initiate dramatic change and disrupt the lives of my loved ones without a vision of where I was headed, or at least a vague notion of a direction?

But enough about me.

As I look around, I see way too many people going through their own versions of what I experienced. I'm surrounded by a ton of people who don't like what they do for work. Depending on the study or survey you quote, 70% of people (or more) are actively dissatisfied with their jobs. Seventy percent! I can only assume that the remaining 30% haven't all reached some state of career nirvana either... my guess is a bunch of them would just say, "Meh," and shrug their shoulders as they fill their mug with more stale office coffee.

I see this as one of the great tragedies of our time. And I have no doubt it is a big contributor to the staggering rates of depression, anxiety, addiction and so forth. I knew that many of the painful manifestations in my own life were largely the result of not being true to myself when it came to what I was doing for work.

Work is too big a part of most of our lives for it to be so-so, let alone a cause for poor mental, emotional and physical wellbeing. If you work 40 hours a week and sleep eight hours a night, you spend over one-third of your waking hours at work! And that's not counting the time outside of work that you spend preparing for work (getting ready, commuting, preparing food, buying clothes, etc.). I was often working 60 and sometimes 70 hours a week at jobs I didn't enjoy. Those of you in that camp are spending about *one-half* to *two-thirds* of your waking lives somewhere you don't want to be, or worse yet, somewhere that literally sucks the soul right out of you.

That's insanity. And that insanity is reality for a staggering number of people.

It shouldn't be this way! It doesn't have to be this way!

I know you already know that. But there's a reason you're reading this. And I'm guessing that unless you're my editor or my mother, the reason is because you haven't escaped the horrible trap yet. So believe me when I say this... I hate to see you suffer. My empathy for you runs so incredibly deep because I know the painful feeling of that situation all too well. I pray that I never get stuck there again. I want nothing more than for people everywhere, and especially you, to have the way you financially provide for yourself be a source of meaning and enjoyment in your life.

This is why I am standing on the roof top passionately shouting this to people far and wide and especially to YOU:

You have to do what you love!

It's too important not to... life is too short. Life is too precious of a gift to squander with regrets. I can't imagine how depressing a fate it would be to reach the end of one's life and look back with the feeling, "I wish I'd had the courage to go for it in life."

It is absolutely possible for you to do what you love. You can make it happen and I want to help.

That's the purpose of this book. This book is about doing what you love. It's about living your unique purpose in life. It's about having the courage to align your livelihood with your authentic self. If you're the spiritual type, it's about making this journey a part of your spiritual path. If you're not the spiritual type, it's about finding something you actually enjoy and escaping the trap of being a slave to a job that doesn't do it for you.

Even the most hopeless people—the people like me who allowed themselves to squander 15 or more years doing something that didn't serve their highest self—even they can turn things around and live their calling in life. Even they can pursue something that gives them a sense of meaning, purpose and deep enjoyment. It's never too late.

I've suffered from just about every cause of being stuck there is, whether it's not knowing what I wanted to do, or not being able to go for it financially, or not having enough time to chip away at it on the side. You name it, I've been there. If I can break free and find deep meaning, purpose and enjoyment, it's possible for anyone.

Not only is it possible, I believe it's imperative. I don't want you to ever be in a position where you look back on your life and feel like you didn't live it to the fullest. I don't want you to slave away for years at something that doesn't align with your true self and fails to fill you with a sense of joy, passion and purpose. It's essential. And it's urgent.

My mission with this book is very simple, and it's ultimately about you. It's about you transcending your limitations and discovering that deep sense of joy and fulfillment that's possible when you're living the amazing life you're capable of living. It's about pursuing your calling in life, it's about finding a vocation that aligns with your authentic self, it's about building a career you can find deep satisfaction and passion in… these are all different ways of me saying the same thing. I might use words like calling, vocation, passion, and so forth somewhat interchangeably, but what I'm always pointing toward is having your livelihood be something meaningful, something you enjoy, something that lights you up from within, something you *love*.

Maybe you don't know what that is yet. That's okay, and you're definitely not alone—I'm very familiar with that territory. There's a good chance you actually *do* know in your deepest core. It might not be a complete picture, but it's enough to get going. It just may not be consciously available to you at this moment. We're going to explore how to bring it to a conscious level.

It's also important to learn how to trust the process and enjoy the journey. Because often all we are shown is the next step to take, and the one after that doesn't reveal itself until the moment it's needed, not a minute sooner. For many of us, that's a new way to live.

Pursuing this path is not for the faint of heart. It takes courage to follow through in the face of uncertainty. It can feel very uncomfortable to step into the unknown, especially if you're at all like I was... somebody who likes to know exactly what you're aiming at in full detail.

Likewise, if you're used to relying on your rational mind, it's a big change to learn how to be guided by your intuition, by your gut, by these quiet whispers from your "still small voice within."

But it's worth it. The risk of not going for it outweighs the risks you face in taking the leap of faith. You can jump, get a little scuffed up, learn from it, dust yourself off and keep going. Or you can risk being part of the masses who "live lives of quiet desperation" as Henry David Thoreau once articulated. I have come to know beyond the shadow of a doubt that the risk of having regrets in life is the much bigger risk to fear.

I can say this with absolute conviction not just because of the massive amount of research I've done over the years, but because I've lived this stuff on both sides of the spectrum and I have the scar tissue to show for it. I've earned my "street doctorate" (to be clear, I am not a doctor, nor do I play one on TV), and I have literally built my life around these principles.

I want to use this opportunity to share everything I have learned about the many different aspects of the journey. Here are some of the things we will explore together:

- What is your calling? What are you aiming at? And what do you do if you don't know what that is? How do you discover a calling? How do you cultivate a sense of purpose and a sense of passion?
- How do you get from where you are to where you want to be? Should you work for yourself or work for other people? How should you start, should you go all in or should you work toward your goal on the side?
- If you're stuck, how do you get unstuck? How do you work through those forces that keep you from going for it? How do you transcend the fear? How do you deal with the risks inherent in what you're trying to do? How do you get over all of those barriers and take the leap of faith?
- What do you do about the challenges that come up along the way? How do you deal with the setbacks? How do you stay true to your path?

This book also contains stories of real people who are on the path of doing what they love. I have learned much from these people and my journey wouldn't be what it is today without what they shared with me.

I'll be sharing stories and lessons from my own experience as well. I have much to share about my many missteps as we venture on from here. But for now, suffice it to say that I know I'm not the kind of person who can punch a clock for a paycheck and be okay with it. I never will be.

I've also come to recognize that so many others feel the same way that I do. And I believe there is no better way for us to succeed in taking this road less traveled than to do it together. If you find this book valuable, I hope you'll share it with others you think may derive value and help give them the inspiration and the kick in the pants to go for it. And most of all, I hope you'll take this journey with me and that you'll share your trials, tribulations and ultimately your success stories.

Let's do this together. The world needs the authentic you. The world needs you and your life as proof of what's possible when you follow your heart, transcend your limitations, break free and live the amazing life you're capable of living.

What is your calling and how do you find it?

What is your purpose? What brings you a sense of meaning? What is something you love, something you enjoy, something you are passionate about, something that lights you up from within? What sets your soul on fire?

That's where you should be headed.

Some of you couldn't agree more. But I can hear several of you from all the way over here. *Sounds great, but what if I have no idea what that is?*

The good news is… you're not alone. The bad news is… you're not alone. The truth is that a ton of us don't feel like we know what our calling is. And if we don't know that, there's a good chance we feel stuck. How can we move forward when we're not sure what we're aiming at?

That was my problem for the longest time. And it was painful.

The one thing that amplified that pain the most was when I would meet somebody who told me "I always knew I wanted to be a doctor," or a teacher, or a musician, or whatever their particular thing happened to be. They were the lucky ones.

True, many of them had trouble figuring out how to reach their goal. I knew people who weren't sure they would be able to get into medical school. I knew plenty of musicians and actors who had trouble "making it." There were lots of barriers that those people had to overcome and they weren't always successful.

But at least they had a goal! I didn't have a goal like that. So I felt lost. And I would've traded positions with any of those people who had a goal. As I saw it, they had the easier challenge (except perhaps for the aspiring professional basketball players). I was convinced I could break through walls, charge up mountains, overcome obstacles, and do whatever I had to do to get to my goal if I only had that goal to pursue. But since I didn't, I was stuck at the starting line, unable to move, but desperately wanting to get away from my present circumstances because they were contributing to some profound unhappiness. So while I sought clarity, I kept working various jobs in Corporate America knowing those jobs weren't what I was put on this earth to do for the rest of my life.

If you're still with me by this point, chances are I'd be preaching to the choir by telling you how painful it is to be spending so many of your waking hours doing something you don't enjoy just to pay the bills. But I do want to take a second to acknowledge that not everyone is wired that way. There are definitely people who are content to work a day job that doesn't fulfill them on a deeper level. It just doesn't bother them. It's the old "work to live" philosophy. A job isn't *supposed* to be fulfilling, it's supposed to support you so you can really live on your nights and weekends.

The problem is that if you aren't naturally hardwired to be one of those people, you might be set up to endure some emotional lows, all the while believing that there's something wrong with you. After all, what do you have to complain about? You have a decent job, a roof over your head, clothes on your back and food on the table. Most people don't enjoy their jobs, right? What gives you the right to aspire to find work you love? It's an idealistic dream.

And besides, not everyone could possibly expect to enjoy their jobs… somebody has to clean the bathrooms or collect people's trash, right?

When people say things like that to me, as far as I can tell, they seem to be brainwashed by this line of thinking or they are arguing for the sake of arguing. To me, it's all just noise. The fact that we won't reach a point where 100% of people love what they do for work is not a very good reason for YOU to settle. If you have to work a job you don't like right now as a matter of personal necessity, that's a different story, and many of us have been there. I certainly have.

I encourage you not to listen to that kind of contrarian noise and instead tune into your heart. Do you believe it's possible for *you* to do what you love in life? And regardless of whether or not that is a priority for everyone else, is it important to *you*?

We all have to dance our dance. What's right for someone else may not be right for you, and what's right for you may not be what's right for someone else. We need to honor this in ourselves, just as we need to learn to give others the freedom to live the lives they lead and to be themselves.

I spent so many years trying to force fit myself into a path that may be right for some, but it wasn't right for me. Part of what kept me stuck were my own flawed versions of the thinking I shared above... "What am I complaining about? Many people would kill for this job."

In fact, I took that type of thinking a step further and made it uniquely my own. It wasn't intentional of course, or I wouldn't have fallen for it so deeply. I love Eastern philosophy and spirituality, and it had been teaching me to be present and accept things. This led to some wonderful personal and spiritual growth. But I misinterpreted the wisdom from those traditions and judged any unwanted feelings I had about work as evidence that I wasn't fully embracing that wisdom. In actuality, my feelings were straightforward emotional indicators that it was time for me to make a change in life. It was only later that I saw that, by ignoring a deeper calling, I was actually stunting the very spiritual growth I had been seeking. If I had listened to my heart, I would have known that much sooner.

Many people who are stuck have underlying stories they are telling themselves that aren't true. Those narratives can drown out what their heart is telling them. Often the story line or belief isn't even theirs, it's something they've picked up and internalized along the way. The particular story line they are believing may be something very different from mine. It may be something they inherited from their parents or their family about what they should or shouldn't do in life... "I should be a doctor," or "Musicians don't make any money." It could be something they picked up from society or from the people that surround them... "Everyone else is getting a regular job." It could even be as simple as "I need this job to pay my bills."

But take a look at that last statement and you'll see how easy it can be to fall for untruth. "I need this job to pay my bills" sounds like a fact. But embedded in that simple statement are limiting concepts that aren't as true as they might seem on the surface. Do you need *that* job, or do you just need *a* job? And what about those bills… have you looked at them closely to see which ones represent essential needs for you? A simple concept we take to be absolutely true can bind us and keep us stuck in a situation that doesn't serve our highest good.

We are all unique and we have to find the path that works for us. I now see that I cannot grow and flourish the way I wish to in life if I am not pursuing what I love and being my authentic self in all realms of life, including work. I know this about myself now. It's a non-negotiable unless I want to go on living an unfulfilling life. The more I speak about it in this way, the more I come across others who feel the same way, even if they might choose different words to describe how they feel.

To be clear, pursuing what I love is not about whether or not everything works out according to a particular set of aspirations I may have. I'm quite certain things will play out differently from my hopes, and I welcome those surprises and challenges.

Instead, the principle I'm espousing is about having the courage to be authentic and to pursue what I feel called to do regardless of how things turn out. It's about the moment-to-moment and day-to-day pursuing of a path that is in alignment with my higher self. It's about staying true to who I am and being willing to take risks. It's about being the person I want to be as I navigate my life journey. That's where the fulfillment comes from. The act of pursuing a calling is what leads to feeling energized, optimistic and content, not the particulars of the outcome.

I love the word "calling." It points to this being about something deeper than our ordinary desires. It's not "I want to do this," it's "I feel called to do this." It comes from a place beyond our small egos.

Who put it there? You certainly didn't. *It* calls *you*. It pulls you in a direction, often without you even understanding why.

Why does one child fall in love with sports, whereas the next child loves art? How is it possible that two children from the same family end up with completely different passions? How come out of the millions of inputs and influences—out of the countless possibilities in life—we feel drawn to only a handful?

It's an incredible mystery. I don't believe it matters if you understand where something like this comes from or why. You may never understand why and you don't need to. What's more important is to honor it. It isn't something you thought up. *It* is calling *you*.

Finding your calling doesn't come from a process of thinking, it comes from a process of listening. It comes from self-awareness and self-understanding. If you want to do something you truly love and you're not sure what that is, the place to start is to understand your authentic self and to bring your livelihood in alignment with *who you are*.

Joseph Campbell encouraged this direction when he said, "Follow your bliss." When you act in alignment with what you feel called to do—even just taking one step in the right direction—you feel a sense of expansion. It may come to you as a feeling of enthusiasm, joy, optimism, or excitement. Perhaps the most direct way to describe it is simply that *it feels right*.

Don't get hung up on these descriptions though. Even the word "bliss" is ripe for misunderstanding, just like "follow your passion" can send people chasing the wrong thing. It's not about finding something that always fills you with fire or consistently feels euphoric. Just like a lasting relationship depends upon a foundation of true love and not those early relationship fireworks that naturally tend to fade, pursuing your calling isn't about chasing an ecstatic emotion.

The direction these phrases are pointing to is this: deep within you there is an ability to discern if the step you are taking is in alignment with who you are and what you feel called to do. The feeling that arises may be incredibly subtle. It usually is. That's why it often goes unnoticed. But trust me, it's there. So part of your job is getting quiet and tuning in for it so you don't miss it.

On the flip side, when you're off track and out of alignment with your calling or your deepest sense of self, you tend to feel a sense of contraction or friction. It just doesn't feel right. Sometimes it can be loud and obvious to you. Other times it's a faint sense that something is off-kilter. Again, it's important to be quiet and tune in to your intuitive heart. That subtle feeling sense tends to get drowned out by your rational mind, which is perfectly happy to grab the megaphone and shout some poor advice in your ear about what it thinks is in your best interest.

So how do you *know* if you're on the path of pursuing a calling?

The truth is that sometimes it will be clear and obvious to you, but there will also be times you feel uncertain. Even if you hone your intuition and get really good at tuning into that feeling sense, you won't know for sure 100% of the time. But in my experience that uncertainty resolves itself if you give it a little time and space to breathe, especially if you begin moving in a direction and getting some tangible feedback through your experience.

One telltale sign that something may be a calling is that it tends to keep revisiting you even if you ignore it for long periods of time. It's as though a calling keeps beckoning you until it catches you at a time when you're ready to accept its invitation. Perhaps you had an idea in the past and ignored it, but the idea keeps coming back. And every time it does, it still has some draw to it. That's a good indication you may want to listen to it. That feeling of being drawn to something is another way of describing that "feeling sense" that I've been talking about.

Again, it's that feeling sense that guides you and leads you in the right direction. It may not tell you in explicit detail: "You need to climb Mount Everest, write a book about it, then come back and start a business selling climbing gear and running workshops for climbers who want to go on Everest expeditions." It might simply show up as the feeling, "I need to climb a mountain." You feel that urge to climb a mountain in the core of your being.

And that may be all you need to get going. Don't get greedy about how much clarity is revealed to you at one time. Most people aren't shown a full picture of where they are headed from the outset. It's not like there is some single destination that marks the completion of your fulfillment in life anyway. So a big part of this journey is learning to live with uncertainty, trusting the process and finding joy in the journey itself one step at a time.

It's just like somebody who decides to backpack around the world without mapping out the trip in advance. I used to think people who did that were crazy (in an adventurous way). Then a friend of mine did it. He left with a backpack and a one-way ticket, trusting that he'd figure out his next step as he went along. A year later he came back with an amazing tale of his adventure across multiple continents and the conviction that the experience had changed his life forever.

How did things work out so well for my friend? Simple. He trusted the process and listened for what he felt called to do next at every step of the way.

Your job is to listen for that next step. Your second job is to take that next step seriously when it's revealed to you. Treat that next step as a "must," even if you can't rationally explain why, and even if you have no idea what comes after it.

But what if you aren't even sure what that single next step is?

That's okay. I wasn't either for a long time. We're going to talk about ways you can go about coaxing that clarity to the surface.

But before doing that, I want to clarify a couple of things.

First, pursuing your calling does not mean you are excavating for the one and only thing capable of bringing you fulfillment in your work life. Your life has the potential to unfold in many profound and meaningful directions. You may feel called to do something today and ten years from now it's replaced by something quite different. You may feel called to do several different things today. Be open to the possibilities.

Remember that *it* calls *you*. It's coming from a deeper place of truth in you. Ask yourself, *am I listening to what my ego wants or am I listening to my highest self, to the universe, to life itself?*

The other thing I wish to clarify has to do with the notion of "passion." It's easy to assume that your calling and your passion will be linked. And while that can be true for many, it's not always in the way we might imagine. Instead of thinking your passion will lead you in the direction of your calling, stay open to the possibility that it may be the other way around. If you begin pouring your heart and soul into something you feel called to do, often your passion for that pursuit grows and matures over time.

That's good news for somebody who isn't sure if they have a passion. It's also good news for the person with too many passions who worries about "making the right choice." Whether you have lots of passions or you aren't sure if you even have one, the good news is that it doesn't matter. Either way, you can start from exactly where you are.

Your primary job is simply to listen for the right next step. So let's talk about ways you can cajole that next step to show its face.

Foundational practices
for pursuing a calling

We're going to start at the beginning and assume you are hopelessly lost, the way I was. (If you're further along in your process, we'll catch up to where you are in a bit.) And by the way, there's no shame in being hopelessly lost. You probably didn't get much help with this along your journey. In fact, most of the incoming messages were probably pulling you off course.

For example, I realize now that most traditional education paths don't do a good job of helping you figure out the most fulfilling direction to take your life. Many educational institutions don't see it as a significant part of their responsibility. How many colleges publish a statistic for prospective students such as the percentage of their graduates who currently enjoy what they do for work? Maybe something like that is out there somewhere, but I haven't come across one. Yet I've seen plenty of schools publish statistics on what percentage of their students got jobs after graduation and what the average starting salary was. Is that really the goal... to get a job regardless of what it is and to measure its quality by how much it pays? The priorities that society propagates, both intentionally and inadvertently, are out of whack everywhere.

It's time to wipe your mind clean of all of its prior influences and biases. And I mean CLEAN. What we need now are totally fresh insights, and those can only come in the present moment. They can only arise NOW. They dawn on you as a recognition that you feel as a resonance in your heart. As with all matters of the heart, soul, or intuition, your rational thinking mind is of little use to you. That logical brain of yours can serve up things for you to ponder in self-reflection, but the actual insight comes from your heart's response to those. So the quieter your brain is, the better. The emptier you are, the more primed you are for this work. The more *here* you are, the more open you will be to fresh insights.

Foundational Practice 1: Meditation

I know of no better practice for quieting the rational mind, encouraging emptiness, and helping you establish yourself in the here and now than meditation. This is the first foundational practice I *strongly* recommend you adopt: a daily practice of meditation.

If you're already doing this, wonderful… we'll talk more about how to use it as a tool to help lead you in the right direction.

For those of you whose resistance I can feel from all the way over here, I'm not going to force you, because I can't think of a way to do that through a book. I'm kidding. I won't even give you the hard sell. I'm not here to spoon feed anyone on the journey of doing what you love... either you're all the way in or you're not.

My point with meditation is simple. If you're not sure which way to go, by definition you're stuck to some degree. That's what being stuck is. If you're stuck, it's time to find out why and how to get unstuck. That can only come through self-observation and insight, not from the same noisy thinking that often gets us stuck in the first place. You need to become reasonably quiet inside and get in touch with yourself. Meditation is the ultimate tool in self-awareness.

If our minds are too full of noise, it's difficult to hear that still small voice from within that's whispering to us. Our minds are loud, harsh judges. Often, that still small voice gets squelched by our "practical mind" which comes in and attempts to save us with its logic and rationalizations.

The answers we need aren't going to come from the level of mind. We're dealing with a deeper matter. Our logical brains will eventually be put to wonderful use in figuring out how to get from where we are to where we need to be once we have the critical insight. But for now, we need to practice shifting our attention away from our busy minds so we can tune into that deeper level.

The amount I have to say on meditation could fill multiple books, and this is not one of those books, so I'll resist the urge to share all of that with you now. There are other forums for you to hear what I have to say about meditation if you're interested. There are many other helpful resources out there that you can check out as well.

For now, I recommend keeping it simple. Meditation is the practice of bringing your attention back every time it runs off to somewhere other than where you are right now. Sit somewhere and get comfortable, close your eyes, and if you're amenable to using the breath as your primary "object of meditation," just follow your breath and feel the sensations of breathing. You can also rest your attention on some other sensation if you prefer, such as the tingling and sensations of aliveness in your hands or somewhere else in your body.

The point is to give your attention to some actual aspect of your felt sense of experience as opposed to the voice in your head. Very soon, your mind will wander. At some point you'll realize your mind carried you off into some fantasy or memory or thought stream. The moment you notice that, gently return your attention to the breath or your chosen object of meditation. In that very moment of noticing, you're already back to being present.

And remember not to judge yourself every time you get carried off, because guess what... mind wandering happens to everyone, sometimes a hundred times in a single meditation sitting. The power of the practice is in coming back every time you realize you've been carried off.

You can also use guided meditations to help support you. This is especially helpful if you're just starting out, but it can be just as valuable for people with plenty of meditation experience because the guidance serves as a reminder each time your attention wanders. There are lots of guided meditations on YouTube, podcasts, on music apps and in meditation apps.

As you get comfortable with it, you can also experiment with meditating while doing other things such as walking. You can even turn daily tasks like brushing your teeth into a form of meditation by shifting your attention away from your mental chatter and tuning into the felt sensations and perceptions of your body.

The most important thing is just to do it. Do it for five minutes a day at first, and then 10 minutes a day. Work your way up to 15 or 20 minutes if you can. Anything beyond that and you're in over-achiever territory. Life happens, so you'll certainly miss days, but try to get at least a few minutes in every day no matter what. And experiment with taking a few minutes periodically throughout the day to stop and check in with your breathing.

Meditation won't always feel easy. It's amazing how difficult it can be to attend to one simple thing. But it's worth it. The benefits range anywhere from, "It helped," to "It completely changed my life for the better." The benefits come in proportion to your commitment to a daily practice.

I'm in the camp of "it completely changed my life for the better." If I could only do one practice for the rest of my life, I'd choose meditation because it's been that transformative for me. Today, my goal is to meditate every day for 10 to 20 minutes first thing in the morning after a cup of coffee. Sometimes I do five minutes. I'm human, so I miss days of course. But I try to do something, even if it's a few minutes, and most days I get at least a little something in. Some days I meditate longer or I meditate again later in the day. I also try to use times like waiting in line or other breaks in the day for a few minutes of practice here and there. Periodically, I do silent meditation retreats for anywhere from a day up to ten days, which deepens my practice tremendously and works wonders when I am dealing with a period of feeling stuck in one way or another.

Meditation is going to be beneficial for discovering and pursuing a calling for lots of reasons, including helping you when you get further down your path of doing what you love. But for now we'll touch on the two main benefits it has for this stage of the journey.

First, it cultivates the right state of mind and orients you toward self-awareness so you're better able to get in touch with yourself on a deeper level.

Second, it can be paired with the reflection exercises we'll discuss shortly, making them more fruitful. In these exercises, you'll be planting a question in your mind that you'll be reflecting on. If you also meditate to settle down and get quieter, you can allow the power of the subconscious to do the work behind the scenes. Your subconscious tends to serve up fresh insights for you during meditation or during the exercise, as well as spontaneously throughout the day.

So there you have it. Meditation is our first foundational practice.

Foundational Practice 2: Journaling

The second foundational practice I strongly recommend incorporating into a daily ritual is journaling.

Research, tons of anecdotal reports, my personal experience, and common sense all point to there being something inherently clarifying that happens in your brain when you put your thoughts to paper. Journaling is another incredibly powerful tool for self-awareness and reflection.

When it comes to journaling, don't overthink it. Just begin by getting your thoughts and feelings down, whatever stream of consciousness arises. "I feel this way…" "This is bothering me…" Do it every day for 10 to 20 minutes.

When you feel inspired, you can pose simple questions to yourself such as "What do I feel called to pursue?" Or "What do I want my life to be about?" Or "What is most important to me?" Then write what comes up in your stream of consciousness.

In a moment, we'll talk through specific reflections you can do to help conjure up from your subconscious the messages you need to hear to help you determine the direction you need to head in. But follow your own intuition as well, and if a desire to journal arises or if a question you are pondering gives you the urge to capture your thoughts in your journal, follow those urges.

How, specifically, should you go about journaling? My answer is to do whatever works best for you and increases your likelihood of following through with it. I keep a password protected file that I can type into on my tablet or computer. I've been doing it for years. There are periods where I journal every day and other periods where I journal more like once or twice a week.

Sometimes I go back and re-read entries. Any time I do that, I come away with insights, especially about things that tend to come up a lot or about my patterns of thinking. It can be shocking and sometimes uncomfortable to see these undeniable, cyclical patterns emerge from the pages. But they reveal something to me that I need to see to help me get unstuck and to grow. I'm usually surprised I wasn't able to recognize them in the moment. For example, I once re-read journal entries from a period of several years and I couldn't believe how often I talked about how much I love creative writing, yet I wasn't making time for writing. Something during that period kept me from recognizing this call back to creative writing. Journaling helped me recognize that call.

These tools—meditation and journaling—are foundational practices that help you build the mental, emotional and self-awareness muscles you need now more than ever. Not only do they lay important groundwork, they can also directly yield insights about what you should do. If you commit to them, these two practices will serve you on the path of orienting your life toward that which you love on the deepest level, both now and throughout the entirety of your journey.

Powerful Questions for Reflection

Now we're going to build on the foundational practices with reflections to help you get the juices flowing. In this section, I offer a set of questions to pose to yourself. These questions are capable of orienting you in the right direction and opening you to the types of insights we are after.

There are different ways you can engage with these questions. We'll talk about why in a moment, but I believe it's best to try all of these methods of engagement.

Engagement Method 1: Write about it

The first way to engage is to write about these questions in your journal. As somebody who has read a lot of books over the years that recommend doing written exercises, I understand if you don't feel inclined to set the book aside and write about them in the moment. (If I'm in reading mode, I don't always feel like shifting gears and taking time to reflect right then and there.) But I trust that if these questions land in the right way and resonate within you, then you will feel inspired to write about them when the time is right. Seize any moment in which you feel that inspiration.

I already touched on how powerful writing can be for clarifying your thoughts. A written reflection also has the benefit of being something that you can revisit at a later time and continue reshaping it until it is the truest articulation of how you feel. And from a practical standpoint, some of these reflections would be too much to hold in your brain at once anyway.

Engagement Method 2: Think about it

The second method of engagement is to dedicate time to intentionally think about a given question. Try going for a walk while you ponder a question or two, or set aside 15 minutes when you're alone to sit and reflect.

The value of this approach isn't just in the active reflection time. Many of us fall into the trap of overthinking an issue, as though we are going to force a sense of clarity to come about through sheer willpower. It can be difficult to stop ourselves from thinking about something we really want to resolve.

But too much ruminating is counterproductive. The mind loves to engage in problem-solving-mode until it comes up with a solution, but this isn't a typical problem that can be solved by the mind in short order. If you set aside time and give your mind the freedom to run wild, then it's easier to create a boundary that signals to your mind that it's time to disengage. So actively reflect, then tell yourself that you are done for the time being and get on with your life. You can always come back to it again later after you've let it simmer on the backburner below the level of your conscious awareness.

Engagement Method 3: Plant the question into your subconscious

The third way to engage is not as common an approach for most people, but it acknowledges the true source of inspiration. Many scientists, artists and creative people of all sorts have pointed this phenomenon out. They think and think and think, and then at some point when they're not thinking, seemingly out of nowhere, inspiration dawns on them. It's the reason it's not uncommon to hear people say that they get their best ideas in the shower or while they're out for a run.

In this third method, plant a question in your mind before a period where your conscious mind is going to rest as a way of priming your subconscious mind. One of the best times is before you go to sleep at night. See if you can have the question be one of the last things you think about before you drift off to sleep. I like to pose my questions as a request for help from the universe to reveal what's true for me or to help provide me with clarity. You could ask for help from a higher power if that resonates with you, or you could simply pose the question to your subconscious. Do whatever fits best for you.

Sometimes you'll wake up and be amazed to find you have a sense of clarity. But even if that doesn't happen right away, that doesn't mean that the process isn't working. Moments of clarity can spontaneously arise at any point in the days that follow. The reason I call it "planting a question" is because it is like planting a seed. It will sprout with time. As tempting as it may be to try to find a way to add more water or give it more sunlight to speed up the process, it can't be forced. Give it room to breathe and trust the process.

Another excellent time to plant a question is before meditating (or before an activity that you find deeply meditative). Often, insights arise in the silence of meditation. It's also common to see things from a different angle during such a period of mental quietude.

I wouldn't recommend doing this before every meditation since it can be very tempting to mentally engage with the question during a practice that is intended to help you turn attention away from that part of your mind. That being said, there are times where meditation creates the ideal conditions for reflection. I like to set aside certain meditation periods to give myself the permission to think about a particular question so that I can take advantage of the clear and spacious mind that often arises through meditation practice.

As I said at the start of this section, I think it's best to try all three of these methods of engagement, even on a single question for reflection. The reason I recommend doing so is because these methods approach the questions using different faculties. Sitting (or walking) and intentionally thinking approaches the question through free-flow at the level of conscious mind. Writing can be free-flow as well, but it also helps provide structure and focuses your mind so you can penetrate a question more deeply with your conscious mind. Both of these methods are like tilling the soil and helping to create the ideal conditions for the seed to sprout when "planting a question," a method that engages with the question at the level of the subconscious.

Now let's turn our attention to the reflections themselves.

What are 40 things in your past that you loved doing?

Look back over your life and think about all the projects, tasks or activities you've done that you truly enjoyed. Catalog 40 activities you remember immersing yourself in that you loved doing.

These can be projects you did at work or in school, or they can be projects you did for personal enjoyment. They can be things you were paid to do or things that didn't pay. You can include hobbies. They can be big things or small things. There's no limit to how far back you should look either.

The main thing is to recall anything that energized you. I know something energizes me when I find myself staying up late working on it because I want to, not because it's expected of me. Or it's something that makes me lose track of time while I'm doing it. I don't even want to stop to eat or turn my attention to anything else. I feel a sense of accomplishment when I'm making significant progress and after I complete it. And I want to talk about it with other people.

It's okay if it's hard to come up with forty things. Do your best to come up with as many as possible. Once you have your list, it's time to reflect on its contents.

What themes do you see? Can you identify common elements across some of the things on your list? Do the things you included suggest any important values you have? Do they point to certain characteristics that make something enjoyable to you? Are there particular environments you thrive in?

Perhaps a chunk of your activities involve working with other people. Or maybe they involve working by yourself. They could involve being outdoors, or working with animals, or working with your hands. They could be things that tap into your sense of creativity, or they allow you to flex your analytical mind. Maybe some are about helping people.

The possible themes are nearly infinite, but each theme is a clue. It's data. You don't need to do anything with this information right now. You're simply getting in touch with yourself, remembering what it is that makes you feel alive and the reasons why. You're tilling the soil.

What are all the possibilities?

This next reflection is a brainstorming exercise. I think it's helpful to do it early in the reflecting phase to open one's mind to the possibilities, but it's also helpful to come back to it again after your creativity has been primed.

In this exercise, set aside time to brainstorm and capture every single idea you have for what you might do for your livelihood. The only filter you have for what belongs on the list is that it must be appealing to you in some way (i.e., "I could see myself enjoying this") and it shouldn't be too outlandish with respect to achievability.

Only you can be the judge of what is too outlandish. (I'd love to say that anything is possible, but it would be outlandish for me to think I would have any hope of becoming a professional basketball player or an astronaut based on my current starting point.) Don't waste your time by including such things, but likewise, don't start eliminating things just because you think it would be hard to make money doing them or because you are an overly harsh critic of your abilities.

Don't overcomplicate this one. Just write down ideas of things you could potentially see yourself doing for work that you might genuinely enjoy. The main goal of this reflection is to begin opening your mind to possibilities. Keep adding to the list. This phase is more about widening, opening and expanding your view. Narrowing and honing comes later.

Once you're satisfied that you have a good starting list, set it aside and we'll come back to it.

What would I do with my life if I didn't have to worry about money and knew I would succeed?

This question lends itself well to writing, thinking and planting it as a seed. The power of this question is in removing two of the biggest barriers that keep us from taking a risk and following our heart: concerns about money and our fear of failure.

Many of us are too quick to discount something because we don't see a way to make a living from it. Likewise, many of us are afraid to take a swing at something and miss. These two concerns are frequently linked.

But if you really love something, that is almost always enough to give you the energy and motivation it takes to get good at it. And getting good is exactly what it takes to be successful and ultimately to make money from it.

So take some time to remove the barriers our rational frontal lobes and our fearful reptilian brains are so quick to put up. Tune into your heart.

What would I do with my life if I only had ten years to live? Fifteen years? Five years?

Suppose you knew that your clock would run out after a certain number of years and you were going to pass away in perfect health. How would that impact how you spend your time between now and then?

Reflecting on mortality seems grim to many, but it's one of the most potent ways to get in touch with what's truly important in life. And it creates a sense of urgency around living our best life *now*, not at some point in an imagined future state—a time that may never come for us. That's why it's been recommended by some of the wisest spiritual masters, philosophers and thinkers since the beginning of recorded history.

I like to play with different time windows with this question because, just as it isn't wise to live on autopilot and assume we have loads of time to figure it all out, it also isn't wise to live with too short-term of a lens. Carpe Diem, but eat your vegetables too.

There is no magic to the time periods I suggested, so adjust them as you see fit. At least for me, as the size of my hypothetical window shrinks, concerns about my livelihood give way to a desire to spend as much quality time with loved ones as possible. So I suggest including at least one time window that is long enough that you would still want to put your time into nurturing a calling, but short enough that you feel urgency to live that time to the fullest.

What am I best at?

This reflection is straightforward—take time to write down all of the things you are best at in life. What are your gifts? What are your talents? What are your unique strengths?

This is also a good question to pose to people who know you well. You can ask friends, loved ones and close coworkers to share with you what they think you are best at. It can be illuminating to see what they point out and it feels good too.

The reason for this reflection is not to suggest that we should only do something that plays to our strengths. Like I mentioned before, you can good at what you need to in order to serve what you love.

But there can be some correlation between the things we're good at and the things we love, and research has also pointed to the importance of obtaining a sense of mastery in driving satisfaction at work. So you shouldn't limit your possibilities to things you are good at *today*, but acknowledging your strengths is another input that can inform your process of self-discovery.

What do I love that adds the most value to others?

This question is helpful in tying together the things you enjoy with things that genuinely add value to the lives of other people. If something adds value to other people, there's a real need for it. Where there's a need, there is the possibility of financially supporting yourself through the endeavor.

The other reason to spend time with this question is because it's important that our reflections not become entirely self-focused. It's important that the pursuit of a calling not become substituted with a simple search for "What will make *me* happy?" Time and again, research and wisdom have shown us how powerful it can be when we serve others. Paradoxically, shifting our focus away from our ego-centered needs toward helping other people has an even stronger impact on our contentment and wellbeing than our direct efforts to make ourselves happy, and it's beautiful for the people we help too.

What do I want most in my next adventure?

This reflection is primarily about the values and characteristics that are important for your livelihood to embody. What are some of the most important characteristics of your ideal vocation? To bring this to life, here are examples from my own reflection.

I would like my next adventure…
- To be something that I truly love
- To be something that genuinely puts good into the world
- To be something I attain mastery in over time

- To offer me the autonomy to set my own goals and schedule, including the ability to work from home some of the time
- To have much lower stress levels than my prior jobs
- To align with my personality (e.g., something that is appropriate for an introvert, etc.)

Your characteristics might look completely different from mine. There are so many things that can contribute to your level of enjoyment while you work—the people, the environment you are in, the subject matter, your daily responsibilities, your boss or your ability to work for yourself, the length of your commute, the hours you work, the attire, and I could go on from here. Even practical and ordinary qualities can make or break your experience. It can be helpful to think back to what you did and did not like about prior work experiences when creating your list of critical values and characteristics.

Once you have your list, rank order them. Usually there are must-haves and there are negotiables. Be clear on which fall into those two categories. It's difficult to have everything you want, but it's important to hold out for everything you truly need.

How do the possibilities stack up?

It's time to begin the process of evaluating ideas. This is not about narrowing the list of possible vocations and trying to come up with an answer. There's no need to do that this early in the process. Evaluating possibilities is itself more tilling of the soil, planting seeds and allowing the subconscious to process all of the information behind the scenes so that clarity and a sense of direction can emerge.

Take out the list of possibilities you brainstormed. For any of those ideas that you feel drawn to evaluate, pose four questions:

- What do I like about this idea?
- What don't I like about this idea?
- What am I afraid of about this idea?
- How much does this idea reflect the values and characteristics I identified in the previous question (i.e., what do I most want in my next adventure)?

When describing what you like and what you don't like, allow your mind to flow freely and jot down anything that arises in your stream of consciousness. Are there more themes you can identify about the types of things that feel most right? Are there any obvious deal-breakers? These are the types of things that are helpful to see.

The third question is helpful because fear and anxiety are the emotions that most interfere with us identifying and pursuing the path we should follow in life. Get used to sniffing out your fears and bringing the light of consciousness to them.

As for the fourth question, one approach is to take the list you created in the "what you want most in your next adventure" reflection and to use them as the criteria by which you evaluate each possible vocation.

When I did this, I rated each of my ideas on a scale from 1 through 5 based on the degree to which they checked each of the boxes (e.g., 3 for low stress, 4 for degree of flexible goals and hours, etc.). I also wrote notes to myself about why I felt that way and any other new perspectives that arose. The purpose of quantifying isn't to imply that the vocation with the most points wins. Again, these are simply tools to get you looking at this question of what you should do in life through multiple different lenses. In the end, your intuition will guide you in the right direction.

A quick reflection on reflection

It is best not to expect that you'll have clear answers emerge immediately from these reflections. That's a possibility of course, but it's not necessary nor is it even the true purpose of the reflections. Again, the reflections are a process of tilling the soil and planting the seeds. Think like a farmer or a gardener—one who is an active participant, but also an observer of a natural process of unfoldment.

So come back to the questions often. If you commit to them, you begin to sift through the noise, the doubts, the conflicting opinions and desires and the thousands of contradictions that exist within you. You begin to hear what your heart is saying more clearly. It may start as a whisper. But you have the power to tune into that whisper.

And I've said it before but I'll say it again because it's that important:

You aren't necessarily going to figure out where you are headed all at once. Sure, there are some people who have a clear vision revealed to them about where they should be headed on this path of doing what they love. Even if that does happen for you, I still encourage you to keep an open mind and heart because your vision and direction may end up morphing along the way. It often does.

But as attractive as it may seem to have that much revealed to you at once, it's not necessary. In truth, all we are seeking is enough clarity and confidence for you to be able to take the next step. That step could be something big like starting a business or quitting your job to go back to school full-time. Or it could be something less dramatic such as enrolling in an online class or committing to spending time learning more from people who work in a field you may want to enter. Either way, you will begin acting on your next step and new understanding will open up along the way.

Three more ways to grease the wheels

Tuning into the deeper call that comes from *within* requires you to get *outside* of yourself. It's a paradox. We only have the power to discern that which our current understanding and perspective allows. Einstein spoke to this phenomenon when he said, "We cannot solve our problems on the same level that created them." We have to find ways to go beyond our normal belief systems, thought patterns and modes of viewing the world.

The simplest way to go beyond our normal perspective is to engage with lots of people from many different realms during our exploration. Find people you respect who are living the kind of life you aspire to live and learn from them. Talk to people who love what they do and ask them about their journey. Talk to people who are working in areas you may be interested in pursuing. Seek advice from people who approach problems like this from very different vantage points—a mentor, a career coach, a spiritual guide, a therapist, friends, acquaintances. All of these conversations can help you see your situation through a unique lens. The wider the variety of perspectives, the better. Remember that you aren't looking for answers from these people. The answers ultimately come from within you. But every conversation yields things that resonate with you and things that don't, which helps to steer you on a deeper level.

The second idea you can put into practice is to travel to somewhere that is very different from your everyday existence (if you have the time and money to do so). Mix with people and immerse yourself in a new culture or way of life. Escaping your usual bubble is a potent "hack" for shaking up your perspective and inviting new insight to come to the surface. There are lots of resources available for how to travel on a tight budget. Even international travel doesn't have to break the bank.

The third idea you can employ if you feel drawn to it is to get in the habit of cataloging the dreams you are having at night. Keep a pencil and paper by your bed and any time you wake up from a dream, jot down some notes to remind yourself what you dreamed. It's important to write them down the moment you wake up from a dream because, as much as you might think you'll remember it the next morning, you usually forget. Dreams can offer another window into your subconscious and can be a reservoir of additional clues.

The primary intent of the three methods in this chapter is to help you see your situation from a new perspective. We are very used to dialoging with ourselves in our habitual way. That's what the thinking mind does all day, every day. We need to spend enough time outside of our typical paradigms, open ourselves to taking in fresh ideas and allow them to stir things up inside of us.

It's useful to oscillate back and forth between these approaches and the foundational practices discussed in the previous chapter. After you've spent time journaling and reflecting and you've pushed things as far as you feel you can for the time being, that's a good time to exhale and engage with other people or immerse yourself in a new environment. Once you've done that, you usually return to journaling and reflecting with new vigor and freshness. Allow the energy of these approaches to build on each other and I'm confident that the epiphanies will come.

The role of trial and error in your journey

At this point we are still focused on the phase of the journey where you're figuring out where you're headed. But this is a good time to point out that much of the "figuring things out" also happens on the journey itself.

As you begin to progress in a direction, you learn from that experience and gain more clarity. This opens up new doors. And once you're moving, you build momentum. Progress leads to more progress. In fact, sometimes the most valuable way to gain traction when trying to discover a calling is to take action and get going on something, even amidst the uncertainty you feel.

Some degree of trial and error is to be expected on one's journey. Many people don't want to hear this. We want to bypass any potential detours and skip straight to the promise land of living our calling. But almost nobody's path progresses in a perfectly straight line from point A to point B.

These detours aren't necessarily "errors" in the usual sense of the word. It's much closer to the mark if we look at the root of "to err," which means "to wander" or "to stray." Some amount of wandering can be a valuable and necessary part of the process. We take some steps and adjust, then we take some more steps and adjust again.

Suppose someone enrolled in school to get their teaching degree. Along the way they realized teaching wasn't going to be a good fit for them, but they discovered they had a passion for education policy. So they shifted gears to pursue that path and they lived happily ever after. Was their pursuit of teaching a mistake? Was it a detour? Or was their movement in that direction the very thing that opened up the possibility of discovering their true passion of working in education policy?

Steve Jobs described a similar idea in his famous commencement speech to Stanford students when he shared with the audience that you can only "connect the dots" of your experiences when looking backwards. He told a story of how he took a calligraphy class in college, and later that experience inspired the typology on Macintosh computers which became the basis for fonts today. But he didn't know that at the time he took the class. He easily could have been sitting in that class and viewing it as a distraction or a pointless detour because the bigger picture hadn't been revealed to him yet. That clarity would only come later.

Open yourself to the possibility that you will wander a bit. It's okay if that happens. It may even serve your future self in a way you never could have imagined.

That being said, it is also possible to make an actual mistake on your journey. Some people's routes are needlessly indirect. My delineation between erring/wandering and an actual mistake is that an actual mistake is avoidable. It is a situation where you have enough of a sense that you're about to move in the wrong direction, but you do so anyway. It's the type of decision that you look back on and say, "I *knew* better," or "I should have trusted my gut all along." You can learn from these mistakes, so they aren't devoid of value. Still, it's wise to avoid these mistakes whenever you can.

My journey has been needlessly indirect because of mistakes like this. I will share more of the specifics of my path later, so I'll keep it high level here as I illustrate this piece of hard-earned advice.

The short of it is that I pursued a path I knew didn't fit because I was clinging to financial security. And I didn't just make this mistake once. There were multiple points at which I actively decided to continue pursuing the wrong path for primarily financial reasons. (I also did this because I didn't know what I wanted to do and I told myself I'd stick with the status quo until I figured that out.)

Every time I made the decision to continue, postponing what my deeper self knew was the right thing to do, I convinced myself I could course-correct later. I'd say things to myself like, "I'll just work through the rest of the year. Then I can pay down this debt and I'll be in a much more secure position to make a switch. What's the downside of a few more months of blood, sweat and tears?" Then the end of the year would come and go and I'd move the goalpost again.

There was incredible opportunity cost to doing that. There are so many hidden costs to continuing down a path you know isn't right.

As an example, whatever the path you're on, you are learning skills that may be transferable to what you do in the future. But if you're on the wrong path, those skills likely aren't as useful as the ones you'd be building if you were more directly targeting your true goal.

When you are building relationships and connections, the same principle applies. These relationships and connections may serve you in the future, but probably not as much as they would if you were heading toward your true goal.

Then there's the mental and emotional toll it takes on you when you continue doing something you know at your core isn't right for you.

And perhaps most costly, it tends to become harder to pull the plug and reset as time goes on.

Now I'm the first to stand up and shout to the world that anyone can rewrite themselves no matter how old they are or how far down the wrong path they may be. I believe that down to the core of my being and I'm a huge cheerleader for that team.

But I've experienced firsthand how it gets harder to switch the further down the wrong path you are. There are forces of inertia at play. The human brain is wired to resist change. It takes real commitment and motivation to override that wiring, especially when you've been on a path for a while. Certain phases of life can also add complexity or barriers to switching, such as having responsibilities like owning a home or supporting a family. And the longer you've been at something, the more you have invested in it, which increases the perceived risk associated with the good things you may be giving up. Success at the wrong thing truly can lock you in forever. It almost did for me.

Every day I spent heading down the wrong path was a day I wasn't making progress toward where I really wanted to be (even if I only had a very vague notion of where that was). Any time you pursue something you know doesn't feel right, you are burning valuable trial and error time that could be spent feeling your way toward your true goal, especially when that goal isn't one hundred percent clear.

So the essence of my advice to you is this:

When it comes to your real goal, to your calling, to your true path…

Always move closer.

Here is what I mean. We are continually faced with decisions. Some are the big ones that are obvious to spot (although not necessarily easy to navigate with this principle in mind). Examples of this might be choosing where to go to college or what to major in, deciding whether or not to take a job or a new role, choosing whether or not to move… the list goes on.

But many decisions fly under the radar because they seem small. These involve how you choose to spend your time on a day-to-day basis, which projects you pursue, what you tell people about your goals and plans, what you choose to say yes and no to and so forth.

My suggestion is that the orienting principle be the same through all of these decisions, regardless of the magnitude of the decision. *Does this seem like it moves me closer to where I want to be or who I want to be?* If yes, great. Go for it. If not, have the strength and dedication to move in a different direction.

It's a simple principle, but it isn't always easy. It's unfathomable how many mistakes I've made. But if you can train yourself to spot these moments and use this principle to guide you, you'll be far less likely to write a book about your unfathomable string of idiotic mistakes a decade or two after the fact. (You can call me in a decade or two and we can compare notes.)

Can you do this even when you lack clarity about where you're headed?

Remember that when it comes to pursuing something that gives you a sense of purpose, all you need is a vague notion of where that might be. If you really listen, if you really turn inward and tune into what self-awareness is saying to you, even your vague, cloudy notion of who you want to be and the life you want to live will let enough light in to guide you. Trust that. Treat even the small decisions like your dreams depended on them. And ask the same question about if it moves you closer. If the answer is yes, move in that direction. If not, be disciplined and move in a different direction. Rinse. Repeat.

Will you *always* move closer? Probably not. Again, your path won't be perfectly direct. It isn't meant to be perfectly direct. What fun would that be? Better to open yourself a bit to the mystery of life, no?

But if you commit to doing your part and always move closer whenever you spot the opportunity, chances are you'll find yourself somewhere you truly want to be and you'll enjoy the journey that much more.

Sledgehammers over the head for the super-stuck

I hope you sense just how deeply I want people to pursue what they feel drawn to pursue.

That sentiment also applies to the process you use to discover your calling. If you feel drawn to a particular approach in your process of self-discovery, great. If you don't, just as well. My goal is to share the raw materials for how you can build your own path to figuring out your next step and to offer some of my personal views on which practices are most essential.

I've saved these last few optional raw materials (the so-called "sledgehammers") for the end of this part of the book for one reason in particular. I truly believe that an ongoing practice of meditation, journaling and soaking with the questions for reflection is plenty for most people to gain the level of clarity they need to move forward, and a pinch of trial and error will take care of the rest.

I also believe that talking to lots of people is a no-brainer. It doesn't have to cost you anything because people want to help (except in the case of formal ways of doing this like working with a coach or counselor), and talking to relevant people is one of the best ways to avoid the pitfalls of pursuing the wrong thing.

But beyond that, we find ourselves in bonus territory. I don't want any of the overachievers of the bunch feeling like they have come up short if they don't do absolutely every last thing in their power to solve this problem of figuring out what to do with their lives.

I feel responsible for sharing the possibilities as I see them and you can determine what works for you. If you are really struggling to figure things out even after wholeheartedly employing the practices we have discussed thus far, here are a few more possible approaches for your arsenal.

Sledgehammer 1: Silent Meditation Retreat

Meditation retreats come in lots of varieties. I only have experience with a couple, with the most notable being Vipassana retreats. I can pretty much guarantee that if you spend 10 to 14 days in silence, meditating a ton every day and having none of your usual distractions (including not even having to plan your own meals), you will come away a different person with some fresh perspective about yourself and the world around you.

That doesn't necessarily mean you'll come away with answers to your specific questions. You can't force insight and revelation.

And a retreat like this can be a challenging experience for some. It's incredible to witness the highs and lows you can feel while spending a week or more doing pretty much nothing. It forces you to face yourself and to confront emotions you would otherwise avoid feeling by distracting yourself.

But I think silent meditation retreats are one of the most highly recommended life experiences. They aren't for the faint of heart, but they can be life-changing and can help you grow in lots of areas of your life.

Sledgehammer 2: Vision Quest

A vision quest is something various cultures and traditions have employed for millennia. It is similar to a retreat, but usually with a heavier emphasis on spending time in solitude and in nature. Vision quests sometimes combine other practices like fasting to support inner growth and transformation. You can find vision quests that are led by organizations or you can architect your own.

The idea of the vision quest is to slow down, unplug from your normal daily grind and immerse yourself in an environment that quiets you and allows you to get in touch with something deeper. The rest is basically magic.

Sledgehammer 3: Guided Psychedelic/Plant Medicine Experience

This one requires some heavy caveats because of its risks. This is clearly not for everyone so please don't read this as a recommendation. I'm simply sharing for informational purposes since I know psychedelics are used by some with great effect for many things, including purposes that overlap with this process of personal discovery that we have been discussing throughout this book.

I also recognize how controversial this topic is despite regaining some cultural acceptance in recent years. I considered leaving it out because of that, but suffice it to say that in a book I want to be as helpful as possible to people in all different sorts of situations, leaving it out didn't feel like the right thing to do.

Regarding the risks, there is the issue of legality in many parts of the world. Even if you travel somewhere to pursue something that is legal in that jurisdiction, you could still be risking your job in your home jurisdiction, and you have to be sure you are doing something like this somewhere that is reputable and safe. As has been widely documented for decades, "set and setting" are critical things to control for, along with many other variables. So being with a trusted guide in a place where your physical safety can be assured is crucial. And being screened for reasons of mental and physical health is equally important. There are many other considerations beyond what I've gone into in this brief word of caution, so anyone considering something like this should do their own research.

Here is why I include this as a possibility for some:

Sometimes the reason we are stuck in life is because our thinking patterns have created such deep grooves in us that it's difficult for us to step outside of ourselves and our usual way of thinking. Psychedelics are extraordinarily powerful in doing just that. They can completely dissolve our usual conceptual frameworks right down to the core of who we are, often to frightening as well as profound effect. (Meditation retreats and vision quests can do this as well, they just tend to be gentler and offer an easier-to-reach "eject button" in the moment.) The power of psychedelics is not to be underestimated, and as I'm sure many would attest, this brief description doesn't do them proper justice. An intrepid person needs to feel called to something like this and to have enough courage to proceed and discover what the experience may have to show them.

Why a guided psychedelic/plant medicine experience has the potential to help some people with respect to this question of what to do with their lives is that it can help them clarify their thinking and their views about their lives on a deep level. This could be as simple as reconnecting with the joys of their youth or opening them up to the sense of optimism, wonder and possibility. Or it could be as life-altering as revealing the answers to their deepest heart's desires.

But you never know what you're going to get. Your experience could be joyful and transcendent, or it could be painful and difficult. It could be a mix of the two. And your experience could end up having very little to do with figuring out what to do with your life. You might end up on some cosmic journey or you might spend several hours reliving and resolving painful trauma from your past. That's not to say that such a thing might not be just what you needed. But it's important to go in with eyes wide open to the possibilities and not to expect it to be a silver bullet. Again, it's not for everyone and anyone contemplating it should do their research.

Sometimes a period of being profoundly stuck requires an extra-strength measure to loosen things up. Having experienced this more than once in my life, I know the feelings of desperation that can come up during such times, especially if the period is accompanied by depression or existential angst. Retreats, vision quests and guided psychedelic/plant medicine journeys have the potential to be extra-strength remedies. They each have their own characteristics and only you can determine if one of these may be right for you on your journey of self-discovery.

A call to action

I used to feel self-conscious about my belief that pursuing one's calling is one of the most important endeavors in life. Very few people around me shared in that belief. In fact, the majority of people I seemed to come across viewed it as ungrounded, impractical and idealistic. In turn, I labeled myself through the eyes of others, seeing myself as a dreamer, as not sensible, as some kind of hopeless romantic.

Worse yet, some saw it as a purely self-centered pursuit and nothing more. *Why should you dare to do what you love when so few people in the world are able to do that?*

It was as though people believed that enjoying work inherently nullifies the value you are supposed to be providing to society. It was as though their unspoken belief was, *It's not the valuable sacrifice work is supposed to be unless you don't like doing it.*

But friends, to this antiquated and misguided view, I offer an equally dated response … Hogwash!

If any beliefs about one's livelihood are unfounded, impractical and ridiculous, it's those beliefs.

Let's take the notion of it being "selfish" and trample all over that silly idea. Philosophers and spiritual masters have repeatedly pointed out a simple truth for millennia—if your cup isn't full, you have very little to give to others. Psychologists will tell you the same thing.

We've all experienced this in ordinary ways. If we're worn down, ragged, stressed or depressed, what we put out into the world becomes a reflection of that. Speaking for myself, when I'm stressed, I'm more likely to be impatient or short-tempered with people. If I'm depressed, chances are I'm spending a lot of my time thinking about myself rather than thinking about how I can give to other people.

On the other hand, when we're filled with energy, optimism and zest for life, we don't worry about ourselves nearly as much. When I am in this state, it's natural for me to give to others. I am a better father, a better husband, a better coworker, a better friend, a better neighbor and a better citizen.

It's obvious, isn't it? Which is better for the world... a bunch of people who suffer through the majority of the hours in the day, waiting for brief respites that they attempt to fill with little slivers of distraction and pleasure before waking up and doing it all over again? ...Or is it better for the world to have a bunch of people who love what they do and love their lives? Who would you rather be surrounded by in life?

When we are pursuing our calling, we discover a passion for life. When we are living with a sense of purpose, our cup is full and we have so much more to share with those around us.

Victor Frankl, the Holocaust survivor and author of *Man's Search for Meaning*, was a living example of how a life of meaning can literally be the difference between dying and surviving in concentration camps. Meaning is that essential to us as human beings.

I used to lament how different I felt from so many of the people around me when it came to how I viewed the topic of pursuing a livelihood of purpose and meaning. Then one day I began to recognize that a lot of these people I was comparing myself to were basically crazy—not crazy in the conventional sense, but crazy in the sense that they had these unquestioned beliefs about the way things are that made very little sense when I investigated those ideas for myself. Many of these people had been brainwashed to believe that work isn't meant to be something you enjoy, that it's all about grinding it out for your nut to squirrel away so that you can one day hope to taste a sense of satisfaction.

And as I looked around, I saw that a lot of these people weren't content. They were living in the future, hoping that someday they would get what they needed to feel truly happy. Or they were living in the past, wishing they could go back to the "good old days" that they romanticized in their head.

Did I really want to be an unhappy, half-asleep sheep following the herd down an unsatisfying life path? I did enough of that to know where that path leads.

But the other path—the path of pursuing a calling and living a life of purpose and meaning—that is where the magic happens.

That's not to say it's easy. In many ways it is the more challenging of the paths. It's always challenging to go against the grain. And then there are the difficulties we have discussed so far, such as the discomfort associated with not knowing what to do next. I have felt the restlessness and the sense of desperation that can come when one is waiting for a sense of clarity.

If those feelings arise, try to find in yourself a kernel of patience and optimism and nurture it. You *will* figure it out. It *will* make itself clear to you. Channel feelings like restlessness into productive action by taking time to execute the practices we discussed in Part 1 of this book. Trust me when I say that those practices can work for you if you commit yourself to them. They worked for me. That is no small feat considering how long I spent feeling lost and stuck before I threw myself into them.

I hope by now you can feel that all of this comes from a genuine and authentic place and that I'm not holding back on you. I want to see you living your purpose and becoming a light for the rest of the world.

So go for it. Meditate. Journal. These two practices will not only help with figuring out your next step, but they'll help you to enjoy the process too. And they'll have benefits in other parts of your life. Take plenty of time in solitude to sit with the questions for reflection. Write about them. Record yourself talking about them. Go on walks and ponder them. Plant the questions before you go to sleep or before you meditate. Talk to people. Ask them about their life and their experiences. Ask them for advice on how to think about your situation. Consider taking some time to travel. Journal about your dreams. Ask for help... not only from other people, but from your subconscious, or your deeper self, or your higher self. Ask for help from a higher power... pray if you're someone who prays (or even if you're not, it can't hurt). And you may also feel inspired to add your own practices to the ones I shared with you. Trust your intuition and act on those moments of inspiration.

Most of all, have faith and trust in the process. In my experience, the universe responds to the quality of your intention and commitment. The more you clarify your aspirations and put them out into the world in intentional, productive and positive ways, the more life answers the call. If you do your part by consistently following through with intention and commitment, the rest will fall into place. It won't be long before things are moving. And that's where we're headed next.

PART 2:

Your Next Step

The Glimmer and
the Judger

At some point something quite mysterious happens on the path of pursuing a calling.

It begins with a glimmer. Out of nothing, out of nowhere, out of pure emptiness… an idea forms. It's often incredibly small and subtle, yet its mass and its impact can be felt without question if we are perceptive. In that instant, we feel a sense of excitement. Our heart starts to beat faster. We feel a sense of expansion. We feel uplifted. This can all be quite subtle, or it may feel very strong, like our mind and body are lifted up in a chorus of "YES." Something about the idea feels right. We genuinely feel like this idea may hold the key to the direction we should pursue next in life.

At this point our mind starts to race. More ideas join the party, building the excitement and the sense of possibility. We know we're onto something.

It turns out this is no ordinary glimmer of an idea, it's the Glimmer. This is the moment of inspiration. This is exactly what we had been waiting for if we were one of the many people who felt lost about what direction to go in life. That doesn't mean all the answers became clear. But all we needed was a tiny seed, and this Glimmer is that seed. We are on our way.

Sometimes in life, people say "I just knew" in relation to finding the person they knew they wanted to marry, or in relation to other significant life decisions. When they say this, they are describing a sense of conviction that can co-arise with moments of inspiration.

This phenomenon can also happen with the Glimmer. It probably happens much more often than we realize, but self-doubt usually swoops in to cloud the sense of conviction. That clouding over can happen a little while later after the initial euphoria fades, or it can happen almost immediately after the moment of inspiration takes place, like a hammer coming down on the idea to squelch it.

Some amount of doubt is to be expected. We aren't all graced by such powerful conviction that we are immediately motivated to spring into action and pursue the message embedded inside the Glimmer. Sometimes the idea we have for what we might do with our lives can feel crazy or far-fetched, so it's only natural that our conditioned minds— which are rooted in maintaining a sense of safety and status quo—will step in and try to win the debate. That's why it is so important to be mindful of this second-guessing. It can hijack your inspiration in an instant and keep you stuck.

The force behind this second-guessing is the Judger. The Judger is the voice inside you that likes to talk you out of what your higher self knows is right. It's the inner critic that tells you all the reasons why something won't work, or why you don't deserve it, or how you'll fail and go hungry, or that you'll let everyone who loves you down. The Judger has no shame. It does whatever it can to keep you small.

All of the Judger's weapons are designed to evoke inner resistance in you. But its favorite weapon of all is self-doubt. Self-doubt is so sneaky because it uses what appears to be sound logic and rational thinking to undermine you from within. The tiniest speck of self-doubt can be enough to deflate you, to rob you of motivation and to stall you in your tracks.

Everyone has a Judger within. So anyone on the path of pursuing a calling and living a life of purpose and meaning must learn to contend with the Judger.

Here is what I believe to be the most effective way to deal with the Judger.

Do not fight the Judger. Do not try to rationalize with the Judger. Do not attempt to outwit the Judger. These are all ways of engaging with the Judger on the Judger's terms using the Judger's tactics. Don't try to out-Judge the Judger. The Judger will prevail.

Instead, the secret is to identify when what you are hearing is the voice of the Judger. Once you see it as that inner critic born from a place of irrational fear, worthlessness and negativity buried deep in our psyches, you have activated your power not to listen to it. You now know that whatever the voice from within just said and all of the associated feelings that came along for the ride are simply not true. They were like the story of a boogeyman hiding in your closet. They were an imaginary scare tactic, nothing more. You can drain their energy and their ability to harm you by simply turning away from them—not with judgment or a sense of pushing them away, which would just be more resisting the inner resistance—but by turning toward higher truths that serve your highest good. You see in the moment that you don't need to live from that place where that inner resistance dwells anymore. You are on a new path and you are committed to taking your guidance from higher truths.

What are these higher truths?

I don't want to spoil too much of this for you, because one of the most joyful parts of this process is experiencing the physics of it for yourself. But here are just a few things I've seen in my experience and that many others have confirmed to be the case in theirs as well.

If you pursue your calling, you are aligning with a force for good. Any time you are a force for good in the world, it comes back to you (and the rest of us) in spades. This isn't some esoteric version of karma, it's practical and obvious. For starters, it makes you feel good in the moment—it comes back instantly. We've all experienced this, such as doing something kind and selfless and immediately feeling good about it. Likewise, it's also easy to see that people tend to reciprocate positivity. Again, we've all experienced this.

So when you have positive intentions, things tend to work out for the best. They don't always work out exactly as you want or according to your expectations, but usually they work out well and they certainly work out better than when you live the alternative way. If you can learn to let go of as much of your grip on control as possible and trust the flow, you will discover a sense of wellbeing that isn't available to us when we are living from that other place.

When I encounter the Judger, I use it as an opportunity to reaffirm what I have seen to be true. I remind myself how my old way of engaging with life didn't work out as well as I would have liked, and it wasn't particularly enjoyable at times. There were many times I suffered a lot as a result of that way of living.

But through my experiences of following my heart and surrendering to the flow, I have been so much more at peace and content. And as a bonus, things have worked out much better than I could have imagined.

To be clear, it's not always smooth sailing. At times, things have felt like they were going off the rails and almost everything inside of me wanted to take the reins and deal with things the way the old me would have approached them. But in those moments, I reaffirm my commitment to this path—the one I know is right for me on a deeper level.

If you've had a Glimmer, it was born from an authentic place within you that is aligned with the direction your deeper self wants you to go. Guard it. Protect it.

But more importantly, nurture it. Act on it. Feed it and allow it to grow.

A first step

For some, the Glimmer brings with it a tremendous sense of conviction about what to do next. For others, the Glimmer is much more fragile and vulnerable to attacks from the judging mind.

If you feel convicted, you're ready to get moving. But if you feel wobbly—the root of which is some sort of doubt—it can be a challenge to take that first step. I'd like to address those who feel wobbly first.

To speak metaphorically, at this stage a single spark has started a tiny flame on a piece of kindling. What it needs now is a very gentle breath as soon as possible to help it catch. Without any breath, the flame will go out. But give it too much breath and it will also go out.

Here is what I mean.

If you had an idea like this, you felt a pull, did you not? It brought with it some excitement and you felt a sense of expansion, right? It wasn't until the doubts came in that the sense of expansion diminished. So now you're left wondering if the initial buzz of excitement was real or if it was over-inflated. Because right now, you just feel uncertain about it.

I'm here to tell you that you know on some level if it was real. Trust that intuition. Sure, it may feel uncertain. It may even feel crazy. But isn't it worth exploring?

If you experience this wobbly feeling, my advice to you is twofold.

First, recall the feeling you had when you first had the idea. Go back to it, particularly in moments of stillness. During or after a meditation is a great time because meditation quiets the Judger. The simple act of allowing yourself to feel that feeling again, however subtle it may feel, is like fanning the tiny flame with a gentle breath.

Second, turn your practical mind to the task of coming up with the smallest step (or steps) that you could take in the direction of your idea. Break it down into the lowest risk actions that require the least amount of effort possible.

Could you do some research on your idea? Could you take some time to envision it all working out and write about what it feels like to have successfully pursued it? Could you talk to somebody who has a history of being open and supportive of you and tell them about your idea and the sense of excitement you feel? (It's not a bad idea to preface what you share by suggesting to them that today isn't the day to play devil's advocate with you.)

Suppose for example that you would have to get trained or go to school if you wanted to pursue this idea all the way through. One tiny step forward would be to look online at training programs or schools and learn about the programs. Another tiny step would be to reach out to somebody who works in that area today and talk to them. These are examples of low risk, manageable steps to fan the flame.

Of course, if you have the appetite and motivation to take a bigger step, by all means do so. But just be aware that if you're wobbly and you set an expectation for yourself to take too big of a step, it can backfire. Because if you take on too much and don't follow through, you may find yourself saying, "Well I guess that wasn't really it because if it was, I would've followed through on that next step." But that is robbing you of your belief in your idea when the idea itself isn't really to blame. You just tried to bite off more than you were prepared to chew based on your current level of conviction.

That's the other half of the metaphor I was speaking about—that's an example of blowing too hard and extinguishing the tiny flame.

Action begets more action. Progress leads to more progress. Action and progress are fuel for the flame. Whether you feel convicted or wobbly, it's important to move in the direction of this pull as soon as possible, and it's wise to set steps for yourself that align with the degree of your conviction.

Hopefully this is common sense. If your Glimmer was to move to a remote part of Asia and teach children English but you felt very wobbly about it, you might not want to buy a one-way ticket and start packing as your first step. But you could certainly start looking into potential places you might be excited to live in. Or you could research relevant 'English as a second language' organizations or programs that exist. Or you could find somebody who has done something similar in their life and connect with them to learn about their experience.

Again, it's about taking action in a way that feels right for you. You need to move forward because that's what builds momentum. No matter how small the steps are that you take, moving forward makes this Glimmer feel like a true possibility. You will start to believe in it more.

There is no right answer as to what your next steps should be. There isn't one single way to proceed. That's why much of the discussion on this topic has been so abstract. I'm trying to paint a picture and evoke an understanding within you to help get you going. And I know from my experience and from what many others have shared with me that once you start moving and you gain a little momentum, the next steps after that become clearer and the necessary doors begin to open.

Enough conviction

At some point in your journey, you transition from just thinking about your idea to wanting to push forward in a meaningful way. Dipping your toe in the water isn't enough. You may not feel one-hundred percent committed such that you're ready to dive all the way in headfirst. But you feel enough of a pull that just thinking about it and taking small, preparatory steps will no longer suffice. You feel ready to gain some real traction.

Some of you may be thinking, "Well that took us a long time to get here. I've been at this point since the beginning of the book." Your challenge wasn't about figuring out what you felt called to do. You've known what it is that you want to do, you're just not sure how to pull it off. At last, we've caught up to you.

Any time you're moving forward and the feedback you're receiving from the events of your life tell you that you're headed in the right direction, just keep going. Indeed, you might not need any more advice or encouragement. We can all be blocked at different stages of the journey, and sometimes the minute we move through our particular block, we are off to the races. The rest takes care of itself. So again, if you're making progress, just keep going. And check back in to share your success story.

But like I said, the blocks can happen at any stage. That's the reason I started at the very beginning and am moving bit by bit through the stages of development on the path to pursuing a calling. And the point we've come to is another common stage we can get stuck—somewhere between dipping our toe in the water and getting all the way in.

At this stage, we have a notion about where we want to head. We have *enough* conviction. We may not be ready to bet the farm on it (although some of us may feel incredibly certain about it). But at a minimum, we believe the pull toward the idea we have is real. The thought of pursuing it gives us a rush of both anxiety and excitement. We're ready to figure out how to make it a reality, because that's the only thing capable of giving us the confirmation we need that this is the right direction for us to pursue next.

A good number of people get stuck here because *this is where things get real*. This is where we arrive at decision points that involve real risk. This is where we have to invest real effort to bring our ideas to life.

So let's discuss some of the questions people face at this stage of the journey.

Should I quit my job or nurture my idea on the side?

To quit or not to quit, that is the question. At least, that is the question a lot of people find themselves asking as they look at their possible paths forward. And it's rarely a straightforward answer. A lot goes into answering a question like this, with your level of conviction in your desired path and the financial situation you are in being right at the top of that list.

We all have to eat. Unless we are independently wealthy, or we have somebody supporting us, or we're prepared to beg for food, we need money flowing in. If jumping headfirst into what you feel called to do was going to immediately pay you as much or more than your current income with zero risk, you could dive right in and we wouldn't be having this conversation. But that's unlikely to be the case for most people.

It's usually the case that your calling isn't going to pay you as much as you are making right now, at least not right out of the gates. And it may be difficult for you to know exactly how much money you will make in the future, or by what point you'll reach a certain level of income. That's especially true if pursuing your calling entails self-employment of some sort, or if you need to go back to school before you're in a position to start working in that new field.

In such a situation, you're faced with a decision. Can you afford to take a risk and go without the security of your current income stream? For how long could you manage without that income? How much are you able and willing to reduce the amount you are spending? And how much risk do you have the appetite to take on?

Again, all of this is a personal matter and it's unique to one's own situation. The good news is you have options. But certain options, which may turn out to be a necessity for some, do require some real patience and perseverance.

Going all-in

First, let's talk about diving in headfirst and pursuing your new path on a full-time basis.

Even if you aren't independently wealthy, or you don't have someone supporting you, or you don't have enough money in the bank to keep you afloat while you ramp up with your new pursuit, that doesn't mean you can't bring your dream to life on a full-time basis from day one.

Because there is one important thing you *do* have right now—you do have some degree of control over how much you spend.

Many people have paved the way and shown us the viability of this noble path. I've known lots of people who have downsized, sold cars, moved to lower-cost-of-living geographies, scaled back their lifestyles in other ways and lived within the means of doing what they love. Yes, it may take some sacrifice. But the one thing I've learned from these people is that given enough time, this rarely ends up feeling like a sacrifice to them.

There's a straightforward reason for this. Unless they're living in poverty, many of the things they sacrifice aren't genuine sources of satisfaction in life anyway. But pursuing a calling *is* a genuine source of satisfaction.

So instead of feeling like prisoners of an unfortunate life situation, they find that their life choice brings them a tremendous sense of freedom. It feels freeing not to have so many "needs." It feels freeing to be confident you can live within the means of doing something you love.

Pursuing a side hustle

Many people *could* choose the path of pursuing their calling on a full-time basis from day one. But not everyone does and not every can. There are good reasons why a person might not find themselves heading down that path.

If you're not in a good position to leap directly into pursuing your calling on a full-time basis, working toward your calling on the side has some clear advantages. The most obvious benefit is that it reduces the financial risk associated with any kind of career change because you have the same (or a similar) amount of money flowing in.

But the benefits aren't limited to ensuring you have income while you ramp up with the new path. It also takes the pressure off in other ways.

If you are depending on your new endeavor to pay your bills, this can push you toward compromises in your decision-making that you might otherwise not feel pressured to make. A freelancer might take on work they would otherwise prefer to pass on. An artist might sacrifice creative purity for commercial reasons. An entrepreneur might be forced to take bigger risks, or cut corners, or raise money in ways they might otherwise wish to avoid. A person who takes time off to go to school on a full-time basis may feel more pressure to take a less optimal, higher-compensating job at the end to pay off debt or make up for lost time.

When you are pursuing something as a "side hustle," you have the benefit of being able to take your time with how you pursue your new path. You aren't under the same pressure to ramp up with your new endeavor by a certain point before you run out of money. You have more creative and artistic license to do things "the right way." You can also take risks knowing that if you fail, you have your primary job to fall back on.

All of that being said, working toward something on the side isn't a panacea. Often you're devoting a lot of your energy and many of your best hours to the thing that's paying you (and to any other non-negotiable responsibilities you have in life). When you tack on this extra effort in the hours you are off, by definition this chews into time you were spending doing other things. Even if the side hustle feels like a calling and you truly love it, it can still become a source of stress. That's true of anything in life that contributes to you feeling over-stretched.

It can also feel frustrating to divide your attention across many things, only to watch one of the smallest chunks of your attention going toward the thing you consider to be your real purpose. Building something on the side truly does take patience and perseverance.

It's also important to acknowledge that some things don't lend themselves well to chipping away at them for a small number of hours per week (and there are things that aren't viable as a side hustle at all, such as needing to enroll in a degree program that is only possible to do on a full-time basis).

There are plenty of people out there who will tell you that this is all a simple matter of you wanting something badly enough… or not. Sacrifice sleep! Go hungry! Do whatever you have to do if you're serious about building your vision on the side!

But I don't think that is a realistic view. It certainly won't work for everyone. In my own case, my day jobs were always so demanding and time-intensive that despite attempts to get something going on the side, I wasn't able to gain meaningful traction. I don't believe this was a matter of not wanting it enough or being unwilling to make certain sacrifices. I also think there are certain sacrifices that are best not to make—particularly the ones that lead to your body and mind breaking down (like cutting way back on sleep) or to irrevocable damage to important relationships. There are other ways forward. It isn't worth sacrificing your health, happiness, or other critical values you have in life.

So a side hustle has its own unique advantages and downsides, making it a path that works for some but not for everyone.

Building a slash career

Another path that can be helpful in navigating financial constraints is to architect your own "slash career," as in being a lawyer/writer or photographer/engineer. While this is similar to a side hustle in that it involves working more than one job, it's not a situation where you maintain a primary job that's a total drag for you or one that sucks up almost all of your time while you pursue your true love with the leftover scraps of time. Ideally, you enjoy all of the elements that make up your slash career. In fact, a slash career is a great way for somebody who has multiple passions to scratch those itches and find healthy balance in their work life.

Here is another way to think about this approach. Suppose you are in a situation like I was… your current job takes up a disproportionate amount of time and energy and it's not the type of job that allows you to reduce your hours to a normal full-time job, let alone a part-time job. Are there other possible jobs you're qualified to do that offer a greater degree of flexibility? Even if this might entail a pay cut, doing so could be the happy medium between pursuing your calling as a side hustle and pursuing your calling on a full-time basis.

I have met many people with slash careers and you'll meet a few of those people in Part 3 of this book. Their slash careers offer them many things—variety in their work week (or throughout the year), the ability to do different types of work

PART 2: YOUR NEXT STEP

that appeal to different interests and aspects of their personality, and even diversification of their income. It's no surprise that those with slash careers are some of the most satisfied people I've met.

Saving up

There is one more method for threading the needle of a financially constrained situation that I would like to discuss, and that is to save up enough of a financial cushion so that you can leave your job outright and dive into your calling. This may be viable for some people, such as those who have a lucrative job or those who are able to reduce their living expenses significantly enough to build up their savings in a reasonable timeframe.

But this is a strategy that comes with some big risks, which is why I saved it for last.

Let's start with something that seems like a straightforward question. How much is "enough" savings for you to be ready to pursue your calling? What's your number?

My follow-up question is, how can you be sure your number won't change over time? What happens when circumstances change? What if new responsibilities come along? Will your commitment to pursuing your purpose hold up? Will you still have the patience and dedication to play the long game?

The fundamental concern I have with the strategy to save up a bunch of money until you can dive in is that you are deferring living your purpose until some arbitrary future state, a point that may come a lot later than you anticipate. In the meantime, you open the door for new hooks to sink into you that keep you stuck on the wrong path. You'll probably get raises along the way, meaning you'll be giving up more if you leave. You'll have invested more of yourself in the intervening time, making it feel more difficult to leave. And your life circumstances may change, meaning you need more of a cushion than you originally calculated.

As somebody who effectively defaulted to this path, I know the risks all too well of having the goalpost move midway through the game while more and more hooks find their way deeper into you.

I am all for saving up as much as you can while you can. Building some runway for yourself is the smart thing to do. Cut back on your expenses. Sock away as much you can. Do it!

But if you're going to save up so you can someday leap into your calling, I strongly recommend doing it *while* you work toward your calling in some way. In other words, at the very least, opt for a side hustle while you're in the mode of saving up. Even a small amount of effort on the side can make a world of difference in keeping you moving in the direction of a livelihood of purpose and enjoyment. And momentum is everything on this path of pursuing a calling.

I know what I want to do, but where's the money?

I have been called many things in life. One of those things has been "an idealist." (I've also been called much worse.) But when it comes to matters of personal finance, it's hard to be anything but pragmatic. We all have to eat!

Because of my particular passions and hobbies, I have known many people whose calling is in the creative arts. This is not a realm of jobs known for having epic salaries. There's a reason the phrase "starving artist" exists. So I've known many people whose purpose in life was doing something that was difficult to rely on for financial sustenance. It's not an easy place to be.

There are people who will tell you not to worry about the money. If you truly love something and throw yourself into it wholeheartedly, you'll become a master at it and the money will come as a result.

I agree with the spirit of that sentiment and it does work out that way for many people.

But it doesn't always work out that way. One need only look at an artist like Van Gogh, whose gifts weren't fully acknowledged until after he died. He's not the only one in that camp.

Even when the money does work itself out, it often takes longer to get to that point than one might expect. We can become skewed by the overnight success stories and forget that the majority of people put years of hard work into their endeavor before they got to the point we see them at now.

Is that a reason not to go for it?

No way! This is your calling we're talking about. It's one of the most important things for you to pursue in life.

But calling or not, you still have your basic human needs. And the joy of pursuing a calling can be offset by the stresses of a highly unstable financial situation. That's the push-pull a person has to navigate.

The question of what to do when one's calling doesn't lend itself well to making money is closely linked to the question we just explored about whether or not to quit one's job. We've already talked about some of the ways you can handle this situation.

I have an affinity for the beauty and freedom of living within the means of one's calling as quickly as you can. But I know that isn't always possible. Not only that, but I am reminded of the story of Einstein who worked his day job at a patent office while revolutionizing scientific thought as a side gig. Pursuing something on the side of another more lucrative job isn't a lesser path. It may require more patience and perseverance, but the degree to which we value things in life tends to be in proportion to the effort and attention we invest in them. It may not come easily at first, but you may find that you cherish it all the more.

I sometimes like to think of this as the universe's way of testing us. How committed are we? Are we willing to give enough of ourselves to that thing that is bigger than us? Not only that, but are we willing to let go and have faith that things will work out? Are we willing to trust that matters like money will work themselves out if we stay true to a higher set of values?

There are no guarantees. Life doesn't always listen to our wants and expectations. It unfolds in its own way for reasons beyond our comprehension. We know this too. But can we hold all of that while staying true to ourselves and following a deeper pull?

As Seth Godin once said, "The world doesn't owe you a living, but just when you needed it, a door was opened for you to make a difference."

Should I start telling people about this?

When you have a Glimmer, that moment of inspiration can energize you beyond belief. As your sense of conviction begins to build, that energy can multiply. It's only a matter of time before it wants to spill out. It's common to feel a strong urge to share your idea and your plans with family or friends, or perhaps with anyone who will listen. We love to share our passions with people.

Not so fast my eager friend! As right as it may feel to share your thinking with those around you, it may be premature.

When your calling is in the fledgling stage, the ideas you have and the plan that is forming in your mind may be a little too fragile to expose it to the elements like that. This applies doubly if you are feeling the slightest bit wobbly.

Any time you share your idea with somebody—especially with somebody you care about or whose opinion you respect—you are inviting them to react. As much as these people may believe they have your best interests at heart, their reaction may not serve your best interests.

Suppose the direction you want to head in is in fact something with the potential to fill you with a sense of purpose, but you still feel some doubt about it. The idea energizes you, but it feels a bit crazy. Maybe it's something very different from anything you've ever done before. Maybe there are a million potential reasons why it might not work.

Suppose you share it with somebody else who points out the reasons your idea doesn't make sense or why you might not like it as much as you think you will. Or maybe they don't pooh-pooh your idea, but it just falls flat when you tell them. Or maybe they try to match your excitement, but you can feel that they don't believe in it the way you do.

What will that do to your sense of energy and conviction? Unless you're somebody who is immune to the approval and disapproval of others or you're somebody who is primarily fueled by proving others wrong (which we'll talk about in a moment), chances are you will feel a little deflated. That's not what you need to be feeling at this stage of your process.

Not only that, but keep in mind that, as much as people want to be unbiased and supportive, there are lots of reasons they may subtly resist your idea because of their own personal issues.

For example, they may project their own risk aversion onto you. They may judge the idea based on how they feel about it instead of looking at it through your eyes. They may unconsciously push back because of a small amount of jealousy you trigger in them when they see you on your path of living your best life, especially if they are not completely content in their own life situation.

Even people who love us and genuinely want what's best for us can subtly resist our personal growth. Sometimes that's because our growth exposes an insecurity in them, and they project that insecurity back onto us. Sometimes it's because the reptilian part of the human brain interprets it as a personal threat, like a fear that person has that you will grow apart and they'll be the one left behind. Sometimes it's simply because people find it uncomfortable when you no longer fit their notions of who you are. Most humans like to have everyone in a box where everything stays predictable. Your growth challenges that and it can trigger resistance in them.

And then there are the more direct consequences your decisions may pose to the people with whom you choose to share your thinking. For example, if they depend on you for their financial security, you may trigger anxiety in them and feel their resistance. That goes not only for a partner, but it could also be the case for a parent who worries about a scenario where they have to step in and bail you out of a hard time.

When you feel anyone's resistance, it's hard not to feel like it's a rejection of your idea or even a rejection of *you*. In actuality, it says much more about them than it does about you or your idea. It's usually that person's fears, insecurities and judgments bubbling to the surface and being projected onto you.

But it isn't easy to discern that in the moment, so there's a good chance it won't feel like that to you. It's more likely to feel like judgment or lack of acceptance. Even if the reaction isn't overtly negative, watching somebody exhibit less excitement than you were hoping for can bring you down a notch. This isn't what you need at this time when you need to be fanning the flame.

91

To be clear, I'm not telling you that you shouldn't share with people if that feels right to you. Only you can decide when it is the right time to share your thinking with different people in your life. I just want to make sure this phenomenon is on your radar. I want you to have every advantage in pursuing your calling, especially in the critical early stages.

Of course, not everyone will react with resistance. You are probably fortunate enough to have at least one or a few people in your life who are as close to being universally supportive of you as you could hope for a person to be.

But even with these people, I still might consider holding off until the time is right. I'll explain.

Throughout your journey, you will encounter people on every part of the supportiveness spectrum. You will know people who are blindly supportive and tell you what you want to hear, which carries one set of challenges. You'll also have naysayers, and you'll have to learn to navigate their judgment and negativity.

My belief is that the very early stages of pursuing your calling aren't the best time for learning to cope with these challenges. The reason for this is not just about avoiding the unnecessary judgment of other people when your fledgling is most vulnerable to the introduction of additional doubt. It's equally about the issue of depending too much on the supportive reactions of others to boost yourself up and keep you going.

The reason I advocate caution in sharing too much too soon is that it is almost impossible for you to avoid gauging the merits of your next steps based in part on what other people think. That is an externally-focused lens. But a calling is about following that which comes from *within*.

Rather than taking on the reactions and feedback of others and using that to justify your direction, to steer you, to boost you up, to stress test your thinking and so forth, I think it's so much more important to take your guidance from within during the earliest stages of the journey. After all, a huge part of discovering and pursuing a calling is learning to listen for those very subtle inclinations and pulls from deep inside of you.

How long do I recommend guarding, protecting and nurturing your calling? It could be a few weeks or it could be a few months. It depends on who it is you are sharing your thinking with as well as your level of confidence and conviction.

In my case, it took me a few weeks before I was ready to share with a few very close and supportive individuals, and a few months before I was ready to share with a wider group of friends and family (because that is how long it took before the majority of my doubts had subsided). And because of the gradual nature of my transition, there were people who weren't in the loop until around the six month mark or later.

By this point, I think I've driven this message home. So now, as passionately as I have advocated for keeping things to yourself in the very early stage, it's time for me to sing a different tune. There's a time to keep things to yourself. But there's also a time to share. And when it comes time to share, it's no longer time to guard, protect, filter, worry about naysayers, or to concern yourself with anything that keeps you from opening up to the world.

When you start putting yourself out there, telling people what you're up to, asking for help, taking risks and being vulnerable, you are inviting support from the universe.

As you talk about your desired path with people and they feel your authentic enthusiasm, many will offer you help and support. They will connect you with others who can help. They will connect you with ideas. They will share things they come across that are relevant to what you are trying to accomplish.

And in my experience, this is when the synchronicities start to happen. Forgive me if I sound too woo-woo, and feel free to substitute the word "coincidences" if it suits you more. But these synchronicities/coincidences start to happen more frequently. It can feel uncanny. The right person shows up at the right time. Barriers are lifted in almost mysterious ways. It can literally feel like you have the support of the universe behind you.

Of course this is also when you'll get tested. How committed to this path are you? How important is it to you to live as your authentic self and pursue a livelihood of purpose and passion? The universe wants to know, and it's not what you say that counts. It's what you do.

These tests come in many forms. A loved one isn't supportive. A barrier arises that throws off your plan. Naysayers pop out of the woodwork.

Oh, the naysayers. They love to troll, to judge, to put you down, to tell you that you can't do it. Learning to press on despite a chorus of naysayers singing in your ear is one of the most valuable tests the universe has to offer. When you weather a storm the naysayers send your way, you come out the other side with a deeper sense of resolve and commitment to this path of living your best life.

Some people like to use the negativity of the naysayers to fuel them. It makes them angry, and they funnel that anger to fire themselves up and do whatever it takes to prove the naysayers wrong. Lots of successful people attribute a portion of their success to this.

Be careful. It may seem to work, but not without adverse consequences. Anger is at best temporary fuel to be used in desperate times. But it's not sustainable and it does damage to you in the process. It's impossible to indulge in it without you becoming negative. It poisons your body and mind. That negativity depletes you of sustainable energy and robs you of your wellbeing. You really don't need it to be successful.

It's so much more effective over the long run to be *for* something rather than to be *against* its opposite. Instead of reacting to the energy of the naysayers and trying to use that energy to slingshot yourself forward, just ignore it and turn your attention to the positive fuel. Tap into your positive intentions, to a sense of gratitude, to your trust in the universe to support you and to the joy that comes from living your purpose and putting good vibes into the world. You will accomplish so much more and be so much happier.

And by the way, the more positive you are and the more good you put out into the world, the more people want to help you. They want to see you succeed.

I know there are exceptions out there. I know there are people who use power, malice, or other negative tactics to achieve tremendous worldly success. I even know they can be surrounded by a ton of people who seem to be helping and supporting them. But the people they attract aren't attracted to them, those people are attracted to that individual's power or influence. They want something from that individual. I don't pay much attention to the exceptions.

Instead, I find incredible inspiration from what happens when you are living your purpose and you start finding more and more people by your side who are attracted to the authentic you and want to help you succeed because of who you are and what you stand for.

So there you have it. There's a time to keep things to yourself and there's a time to share. When it's time to keep things to yourself, cultivate your intuition. Listen to the still small voice within. If it's truly the right direction to steer your life in, your heart will provide you with all of the fuel you need to build your momentum and conviction.

And once it's time to share, let your guard down and share as freely as you can. Let the negativity you encounter slide off of you. Don't give it your attention. Pay much more attention to the almost magical way things begin to take form around you. I call it magic because any of us can plainly see how little control we have in life, yet something that begins as the tiny seed of a Glimmer can grow into a magnificent life of contentment.

Most importantly, consistently reaffirm your commitment to that which is most important to you—to living a life of authenticity and purpose, to living without regret, to having the courage to go for it in the face of uncertainty and challenges, to trusting the flow of life and to enjoying the journey itself. You are on the path, and it feels incredible to be on the path.

PART 3:
Real People and the Leap of Faith

Diving into the unknown

We've come to the pivotal point of the journey—the moment when you are standing on the precipice of a high dive into the unknown. It's energizing. It's scary. It may be one of the most challenging things you ever do. But it holds the possibility of tremendous growth and satisfaction and it has the potential to change you forever.

The thing about it is, eventually you just have to go for it. You have to pursue a direction you feel called to pursue in the face of a million unknowns, even if it feels crazy.

There's really no "how" when it comes to doing this. There's no guide book. There's no step-by-step process to follow. "Go for it." "Take the plunge." "Trust the process." These don't tell you *how* to do anything. *How* does one "trust the process?" You learn by doing it.

You either take the leap of faith or you don't.

When writing a book devoted to encouraging you to follow your calling and helping you navigate the terrain, it's uncomfortable for me to come to a point where there is little to say in the way of "how-to." I also experienced the challenge of this in my own journey. I approached the precipice, wanting nothing more than to abandon the path I was on and throw myself into a new life of purpose and meaning.

But more than once, I came to that precipice and backed away.

There were a lot of reasons for this, but I believe one of the reasons was that I was surrounded by too many people who were stuck on the same path I was. I didn't have the living examples in my own life of people close to me who were embracing the risk and taking the road less traveled.

So when I finally saw that I needed to find a way to change the direction of my life once and for all, I went looking for a new kind of help. I could see that the main thing standing between me and a livelihood I could truly love was me, that nobody could tell me exactly how to do it, and that I needed to traverse the terrain myself. But inspiration can be a powerful catalyst, and one of the most potent forms of inspiration is to surround oneself with people who have done that thing you aspire to do.

So I began seeking out people who had taken the risk in their own lives to pursue a calling. I reached out to people I knew, people I had heard about but had never met, and soon those people were connecting me with others who they knew were on the path of living their purpose. I met with dozens of people in coffee shops, restaurants, bars, on the phone and in airport terminals. I listened to their stories. I absorbed their trials and mistakes, their failures and successes, and the lessons and advice they offered to me and to everyone who feels drawn to taking this journey.

Most importantly, their energy lit a spark inside of me.

Since writing is a love of mine and it's a tool I rely upon for my own reflection and personal development, I also asked for permission from some of these individuals to share their story with others.

I've written many things in my life, but nothing feels as high-stakes as sharing someone else's story. This is especially true when it is somebody for whom you have tremendous respect. I have done my best, but I know these vignettes are incomplete, imperfect, and subject to the limitations of my own perspectives and ability to communicate.

I'm also aware that they are skewed toward people who have pursued a particular flavor of path in life—lots of slash careers, lots of creative endeavors and a good deal of self-employment. As I said, I'm sharing the actual stories I sought out at the very point I came to my own precipice, so they reflect some of the elements of my own aspirational path in life. In a way, that makes them all the more authentic and real. These people and these stories are what pushed me over the edge.

I have made peace with the degree to which I have come up short in selecting for variety of life path because of how much I have seen that the core themes are common to just about any flavor of life path. Indeed, the more people I spend time with going deep on this topic, the more I realize that the particulars matter very little. It's about the wisdom and the lessons, and it has surprised me how consistent they are across the range of people's life experiences.

And to the degree I've come up short in my telling of the stories, I've made peace with that through the amount of leverage I've gained (and shared) as a result of these people and their generosity. It's been quite some time since I had some of these conversations, yet I still think of all of these individuals often, and I reference them frequently when coaching others who are on the path of pursuing an authentic livelihood. I owe each of these individuals such gratitude for how much they influenced the direction of my life and other people's lives as well. I am excited for their impact to continue to echo and spread.

So without further ado, let's dive into stories of real people who have taken the leap of faith and pursued a calling. I hope they serve as a catalyst for those of you in need of one, just as they have for me. And perhaps one day your story will be the catalyst for others who feel that they, too, need to take the risk to follow their hearts and pursue a livelihood of purpose, meaning and passion.

The difference between passion and purpose

This was the day. It was five years in the making, but also a lifetime in the making.

For the last five years, Jon Allegretto had been working at the auction house. It was fine work. There were good people there and they were generous to him. But the work was repetitive and time moved much slower while he was there. It wasn't the kind of slow that makes you stop and appreciate things, it was the other kind of slow—the kind that makes it feel like a part of your spirit is slowly draining through a tiny hole in a bucket one drop at a time.

Every drop was another reminder of how he wasn't serving his purpose. Whenever you slow the frames down enough, this kind of thing tends to stare you right in the face. Drip. Drip.

For those five years, and plenty of years prior to that, Jon had been nurturing one of his passions on the side—as a musician, playing in a rock band. But not many people make it in that line of work. The truth is, not many even give it a real try. And most of those who do go for it end up getting swallowed up by late nights, by long stints on the road, by the industry, by the lifestyle, by not achieving the success they want, by running out of money, by burnout.

But here's the thing. If it's a calling, it doesn't listen to all of those reasons to stay away. It just keeps calling. You can try to push it to the back of your mind or ignore it, but it doesn't go away. It might go dormant, but whenever things get quiet enough, there it is again, calling, patiently waiting for you to pay attention.

And if you listen and you decide to follow it, you eventually find yourself at the pivotal moment.

Jon's moment was at the auction house, there for the last time in his life, about to cut the cord and leap into the unknown. No more relying on it for safety. This was it.

He said goodbye and walked out of there one final time. As he got outside, he balled up the pair of pants he had worn as part of his uniform for the job and tossed them in the dumpster.

At this point in Jon's story, I was rapt. I felt the tension he must have felt. I asked him what was going through his mind at that exact moment of cutting the cord.

"It was 'F*%#... now what?'" he said.

"Why the pants in the dumpster?" I asked.

He looked under the table. I was puzzled.

"Okay phew," he said after he had positive confirmation on what kind of pants I was wearing. "Because I *hate* khakis. I vowed I would never wear them again in my life. I still haven't."

I quickly came to find out Jon had a tremendous sense of humor and an infectious personality. But he also had incisive perspective... the kind where he would drop something on you that was so profound, you could see there was a depth to him that would take years to get to know.

The evening we spoke, Jon and I were sitting in a bar in Wicker Park, a bustling Chicago neighborhood. As I sat listening to him share stories about his life, I couldn't help but become introspective about the mystery of the paths we all take.

Years before this conversation, I moved south to the mid-Atlantic to escape northern winters, only to end up in the Chicago area after getting married. Jon's reason for being in Chicago was that he had followed an inner urge to move away from his home town of Williamsburg, VA to a big city that wasn't New York or Los Angeles. As he was contemplating his move, he told me how all kinds of signs started pointing him toward the Windy City until he was sufficiently convinced the universe was conspiring to get him there. Then he *knew* he had to go.

So there we were, two people who had no logical reason for crossing paths in life, one of us having bounced haphazardly toward this moment (me), the other having followed his vision and his intuition (Jon). The more we spoke, the more it was apparent to me that this was how Jon approached all of his life.

At one point Jon told me, "If I'm doing the wrong thing, I know it."

When he said that, I wondered what it would be like to have that degree of inner vision. I knew I could learn a lot from Jon. But it would be years before I began to tap into my own intuition like that.

Jon *knew* when it came to something else even more foundational to his life than his decision to move up north. He recalled being about three years old when it started. He begged his parents for something over and over again, and it wasn't a Lego set or toy trucks or a puppy. It was a guitar.

His parents resisted. He continued asking them for a guitar for years. It wasn't until he was twelve years old that his parents finally caved in and bought him one. It took Jon falling deathly ill and being hospitalized before they softened up about the idea.

Since the beginning, music has always been a central part of his life. Sometimes you get a glimpse into how deep something runs in a person. At one point in our conversation, Jon dropped a bomb on me about how, recently, three of his friends had tragically passed away. But almost in mid-sentence a song came on and he cut himself off to announce to me, "This is Henry Rollins band!" He abandoned the story about his friends in favor of some air drumming for a few seconds and explained to me what a huge influence Henry Rollins band had been on his life before returning to his previous thread.

Jon began writing music the minute he started playing. Not only that, but he recorded everything he ever wrote—songs, short little riffs, anything he wanted to remember—and he kept everything from the earliest days of composing (his earliest stuff was still on cassettes).

This love for music brought him to solo music, to his band *A Friend Called Fire*, to a series of self-organized national tours, even to playing on one of the stages at Madison Square Garden.

For years, Jon was able to pursue all of this while working at the auction house, including touring with the band. It was one of the unique aspects of his job and the people there—they gave him the flexibility to take a bunch of weeks off at a time for a tour. Not many jobs would still be there waiting for someone after a national tour. So why quit?

Again, it came to his sense of intuition… to the quiet, wise voice from within. It told Jon he was becoming too reliant on it and it was time to move on. So he listened.

But things rarely move as quickly as you want them to, and there are bills to pay from day one. So Jon started stringing together various sources of income. There were a bunch of different odd jobs. He spent some time working from home for a tech company. He taught guitar lessons. He also taught a higher education class at an art school.

But most importantly, there was his photography, something we'll come back to in a minute.

As a quick aside, many people I have talked to who have gone for it and pursued a calling in life have shared with me that this period in their journey was the most difficult. The leap itself can be scary, but it's short-lived and there is usually energy and optimism to balance out the anxiety.

But the period directly after the leap has a different quality to it that can make it uniquely difficult. Yes, there is fear due to the practical, financial reasons. Yes, there is often the added stress of working harder than usual at this stage. But the difficulty comes from another source altogether. Often, this is when self-doubt is at its strongest. As soon as you layer the toxicity of self-doubt onto this collection of forces, you have a perfect storm. Many have told me that they felt like others couldn't relate to the difficult feelings they were going through during this phase of their journey, and that realization brought on a deep sense of loneliness... like they were on an island all by themselves.

It's hard enough to get through a difficult phase in a journey. But to do so while you feel alone is a different beast altogether. As people shared similar stories with me, I was reminded of a quote by Hugh MacLeod. "The price of being a sheep is boredom. The price of being a wolf is loneliness. Choose one or the other with great care."

Jon had made his choice, and he quickly found that he was experiencing this medley of difficulties. As he described the challenges he faced during this early phase, he told me that in his case, it could have dragged him down further than it did had he not been so fortunate to have a strong support system. The center of this was a woman he was in a relationship with at the time who was a tremendous grounding and encouraging force in his life. She helped keep him positive, going above and beyond to consistently remind him that he would be alright and things would work out.

In time, Jon began to get his footing. And a big part of it was by returning to another passion of his—photography. Jon had gone to school for journalism and had a strong background in photography, but it wasn't the sort of profession that a person can jump into and have a stable income stream from day one.

But after leaving the auction house, Jon was on a new path and he threw himself back into his photography by shooting for weddings and other live events. He began to get busier and in time, photography was a legitimate income stream.

When I took a look at Jon's work, it was easy to see that he had as much of a gift for photography as he did for music. And it came as little surprise to me when he told me his portfolio included doing photos and editing for live events like Zac Brown Band shows and many others. Who better to shoot live music events than a musician/photographer?

As I talked to John, I could see how much this slash career made sense for him. I wanted to know more about the nuts and bolts of supporting himself through his two passions. He explained to me that one of the downsides of being a performer and doing photography is that they both "peak in the summer and are like tumbleweed in the winter."

But on the bright side, he told me that the photography pays pretty well and provides balance to his life—balance that offsets the potential for burnout he acknowledged he might feel if he focused exclusively on music.

The income from Jon's music wasn't limited to what he earned from his own recording and the shows he and his band did. He also took on other music-related side jobs to supplement his income including doing commercials. (One of those commercials was Coca Cola's *Taste the Feeling* campaign, which I was able to find online. John was in the chorus.)

I asked Jon about how he felt doing ads like that since I was aware some musicians have a thing about doing music for purely commercial reasons rather than for the purity of the art.

Jon's response was, "If you're doing music professionally, you are providing a product to people, and part of that needs to be kept in mind. There are lots of ways to monetize your art without compromising your integrity and beliefs. You also have to survive. I've heard people say things like, 'Talk about selling out, I heard Led Zeppelin in a car commercial...' But for me, if they wanted to use my song in a car commercial and they're reasonable about it, I'd be like, hell yeah, let's go."

His attitude seemed to me to be *whatever it takes*, and it resonated with me. You can pursue a passion for yourself, but if you choose to survive off of it, you have to be realistic about how much it's just for you and how much it's for others too.

And in Jon's case, he was doing exactly what he wanted to be doing with his life—music and photography. Yes, he has aspirations. He wants to grow and reach new levels in both of these art forms that he loves so much. But he wanted to be doing exactly what he was doing in that moment. He seemed content in a way few others I had come across in life were when it came to his livelihood. That is an amazingly rare thing, something I hope changes for the rest of us on a large scale.

I learned a ton from Jon. It would be difficult to capture it all in such a brief vignette. But there is a particular reason why I chose to share his story first.

Jon was one of the earliest people I met with when I began seeking guidance, inspiration and frankly a catalyst to help me shift the trajectory of my professional life. I kept referring to his music and photography as a "passion," just as I have done at various points in sharing this story.

But the deeper I went with Jon, the more I understood why the importance of "following your passion" has been the source of debate when it comes to finding satisfaction in one's livelihood.

To be clear, there has never been any question in my mind that music and photography are passions of Jon's. But the more we talked, the more I came to see that there was something even more fundamental about these pursuits to him.

At one point he told me, "I don't have a choice not to do it."

And at another point, he said something that really got my attention:

"I have the belief that music is somewhat divine, like I have a *responsibility* to do it."

Something profound struck me in that moment he used the word *responsibility*. I had a moment of true clarity. I suddenly realized the important difference between *passion* and *purpose* on this journey of doing what you love. It's not that passion isn't important and valuable. But at a fundamental level, passion is more about how something makes you feel. Responsibility, on the other hand, that's an entirely different thing.

I feel I have a *responsibility* to be the best parent I can be. It's not the kind of responsibility one laments, like my responsibility to pay my mortgage. It's a different kind of responsibility, the one Jon was speaking about. When we feel this kind of responsibility, it's as though we've been given this gift that we have to care for and honor, and we know we would not be living our best life if we fail to follow through with that.

To me, that's what separates a calling from an ordinary desire. It's that clarity of purpose. On a practical level, it feeds this incredible persistence, this attitude of I will go through, over, around... whatever it takes to get to the other side of these mountains.

That's something Jon has that not everyone has. Not everyone has the will to traverse the ravines of adversity. And passion alone can only take you so far. It becomes an entirely different journey when it's about discovering what brings you a sense of purpose.

When talking with Jon, it's almost as though I forgot about the practical day-to-day challenges. I had few doubts about his ability to make it work over the long haul. These pursuits ran so deep in him. He gave himself no other options but to make it work in one way or another. That's how much clarity of purpose I saw in Jon.

That clarity of purpose helps in innumerable ways. But it doesn't take away the challenges of the journey. One still has to invest incredible energy to get to the other side of those mountains. One still has to find a deep reserve of patience and persistence. And one still has to deal with the pain of sacrifice.

Jon has made many sacrifices along the way. He gave up the security of steady employment. He had to make adjustments to his life to make ends meet. He went against the grain, choosing not to take the safe route, even if others in his life would have preferred that he do just that. He could have listened to his parents' anxieties. He could have listened to that voice of the Judger that says things like "you'll end up starving on the streets."

There were also the sacrifices we didn't talk about, the ones he chose to keep close to the vest. He vaguely mentioned "knowing at one point that it was not the right time for certain changes in [his] life," and then he shared no more. I imagined a relationship on the verge of moving to a deeper level of commitment, but ultimately ending in the two of them parting ways because it would go against this path he had chosen to take. I may never know. But the sacrifices a person doesn't want to talk about tend to be the ones that were the most difficult to make.

Having a sense of purpose doesn't eradicate doubts about exactly what one should be doing. True, Jon had the clarity to stay the course with his music and photography. But the more specific choices within those realms carried just as much uncertainty as anyone else's journey.

For example, he told me one of his biggest struggles was, "Should I spend my time doing this or that?" There are so many possible directions he can go. He can go all-in on one thing, or half-in on a couple things, or a little-less-in on three things, and there aren't always clear signs about which approach is best.

As clear as your sense of purpose can be, there is still the need to navigate those decisions. There are still the doubts that arise about whether or not you've made the right decision or you've stepped off-track. As I shared earlier, often the best you can do is simply to embrace the philosophy of *always move closer*.

Jon described his approach to this in his own words—as a constant process of honing and redirecting, of looking at things and saying, "What will I do of the things I enjoy, and how do I cut off more of the fat?"

When talking with Jon, I felt like I could've been sitting across from somebody 20 or 30 years older sharing their life wisdom with me. I saw the patience. I saw the surrender to what can be a much more gradual process than most people realize. But I also saw a conviction—that there really is no other way.

When I asked him for parting advice, this is what he shared:

"If you don't pursue your goal one hundred percent of the way your way..."

And he left it at that. We're left to fill in the blanks ourselves.

Leap first

Have you ever met someone who instantly changed your perspective and helped you to see the world in a new way?

Not everyone finds their way into my thick skull. But Jennifer Bachelder tiptoed right in there and did something to my brain that I never undid.

It started with the simplest of things. We met at Starbucks. I ordered an iced tea. I took the straw out of the wrapper. Without realizing it, I proceeded to do this nervous twitchy thing that I have probably been doing every time I have ever been with another person at Starbucks.

I wound the wrapper around my finger and then unwound it over and over about 100 times. Considering all the times I've been to Starbucks and ordered an iced tea, I've probably wrapped that thing around my finger fifty thousand times.

At one point in our conversation, Jen picked up the now curly wrapper that was sitting on the table and asked me, "How many people and how many hours went into making this?"

I sat with a blank stare.

She proceeded to list out for me all of the things that probably had to happen to bring that wrapper to fruition.

People deciding on the color. People approving the decision to spend more on something in color instead of black and white. People approving the color to make sure it was consistent with the brand. People approving the font. People choosing the words that would be printed. It's a cautionary message, so legal probably got involved...

She went on. All of this money, energy and people's time spent on some little thing that ends up in the trash. Or in this case, it's mindlessly wound around someone's index finger a hundred times and then ends up in the trash.

I had never seen anyone speak passionately about a straw wrapper before. I probably never will again.

For me, it started with that wrapper, but it quickly spread. I started noticing things. All over the place, that day and ever since, I have been noticing things that I never would have noticed had it not been for meeting Jen.

It turns out that Jen has a soft spot for trash.

In college, Jen majored in graphic design. In one of her classes, the professor did something that hit her hard, probably harder than she even realized at the time. After everyone submitted their final projects, something they had all worked tirelessly on for a ton of time, he walked around the room with a trash can and made every single person throw their project away. He was teaching everyone a lesson about where a lot of their work was going to end up given their chosen profession.

Since then, Jen has paid attention to things that end up in the trash.

Fast forward several years: Jen was getting a lot of junk mail in her post office box. She started turning the junk mail into postcards that she would then send to her friends. She got a kick out of turning that trash into something and then having the post office deliver it all over again. Eventually, that turned into a side project in postcards, which later expanded into designing calendars—first as gifts for her graphic design clients, but pretty soon she was selling more of them than she was giving away.

And then there's her studio art. She focuses primarily on turning garbage into art. That happens to be the opposite of my usual approach, which is to try to make art but instead to make garbage.

These days, Jen's friends are now all well-aware of her soft spot for trash, so they save trash they think she might like and give it to her, which made her think...

If I'm even making people take notice of trash for one second before throwing it away and having it end up in a landfill, perhaps there is something meaningful there.

It's quite the evil plot to infect innocent people like me. It worked. I've already sent hate mail to her college professor, made out of some torn up credit card offers and the flyers for lawn care services that get wrapped around my front door knob daily.

But let's back up. Because what first attracted me to Jen's story was something entirely different.

Not too long ago, Jen had a "regular job" at a marketing company as an event producer. There she was—a graphic designer by training and someone who probably would have pursued studio art if she was "more of a risk-taker and had more confidence in [her] studio art skills." But she was in the events business, which wasn't something that spoke to her. Not only that, but she was doing events for a Horrible Boss.

(My words, not hers, so the hate-trash-mail can come to me, not her.)

She knew she had gone off track. She knew fear had gotten the better of her.

It hadn't always been that way. Her ideal job coming out of college was to design album covers for a record label. She snagged an internship doing just that at Invisible Records, an industrial metal record label. To make ends meet, she worked part-time as a babysitter, she worked part-time in a flower shop and she slept on her friend's couch.

After some time, Jen decided to take a job at this marketing company. She started off doing both graphic design and events. But after a few years, she was promoted to the head of the events department. In this role, she worked for a boss who cyclically went through episodes of projecting all of his problems onto everyone around him and then firing a bunch of people.

Jen knew it was time to move on. It wasn't just the boss. The problem was that her artistic passions and freelance design projects were being crammed into the tiny windows of free time she could scrape together during nights and weekends, whereas she was spending the vast majority of her best waking hours working on something for someone else that just didn't excite her. And she suffers from what I call Overachiever Syndrome—the inability to do anything less than A+ work. She pours her heart into everything, even if it's not really what she wants to be doing.

So Jen did something a logical and pragmatic person would do, and she put together what I will refer to as a Super-Practical-Six-Month-Plan to save up money and make the leap into doing her passion full-time—her graphic design and studio artwork.

If you ever find yourself in a similar situation—working a day job you don't like while pining for a full-time career doing something you love—I encourage you to reach out to Jen for advice on the nuts and bolts of assembling your own Super-Practical-Six-Month-Plan. In the meantime, I've distilled the essence of her overarching approach into a few key steps, which are as follows:

1. Get out a pen and paper.
2. Write down a super practical plan for how to save up enough money in six months to leap from your current job into the profession of your dreams.
3. Spend one extra second taking notice of this piece of paper before dumping it into the trash.

Three weeks after Jen hatched her master plan, she and her boss had a "disagreement." Given her definitively warm and witty personality, I can only guess who may have been the instigator.

But when the time is right, the time is right... even when the time isn't really right according to the plan you put together and sent to the landfill.

So Jen abruptly quit, moved back to where her family lives in Ohio, and rented out half a duplex from her new landlord, her younger brother.

As a quick aside, the writer and entrepreneur Seth Godin gave a talk that was turned into an audiobook called *Leap First*. I highly recommend it. And I think "Leap First" is an appropriate tagline for Jen's journey.

The "leap first" approach definitely isn't for everyone. But I think Jen is a living example of why it can be an effective approach for some people when pursuing their purpose in life. (My lawyers are telling me to include a disclaimer: I am not responsible for any loss or damages should you choose to follow this approach.)

Here's the thing with Jen's leap. I wouldn't pretend it was or is easy for her. She worked her tail off. Especially early on before she had grown things to a point where she could be more selective about the work she took on, she had to work with difficult clients she would have preferred to fire and to say yes to projects she would have loved to pass up.

To supplement her income, she allowed a revolving door of strangers into her home by renting out part of her place through Airbnb. (Ironically, her place was very close to an Airbnb call center, so it became a hotspot for Airbnb employees who happen to make very good Airbnb tenants.)

And self-employment isn't always easy in other ways, particularly when you're early on and working your way up. Jen shared how she had difficulty making time for self-care, such as getting enough sleep or having time to squeeze in workouts. She also spoke to me about the inherent uncertainty, like clients who don't pay on time and the risk of clients who don't pay at all.

But compare this self-employed path to her life as an event producer. At the time we spoke, she was working about 30 hours a week freelancing as a graphic designer for a few primary clients. In her remaining time, she was devoted to her passion for studio art as well as growing a budding business doing projects like wedding invitations, the postcards I mentioned earlier and much more.

She designed a slash career that spoke uniquely to her. Studio art is about creating something for herself. Graphic design is about bringing a client's vision to life. Studio art is a solitary activity, whereas graphic design gives her much needed interaction with people and the associated creative inspiration that helps keep her studio art fresh. She doesn't actually want one of these two careers to win out; she likes a balance of the two.

It's so obvious when you spot somebody who is doing something they are meant to be doing. For starters, she is amazing at what she does. She has a gift very few people have when it comes to client work. I got a taste of it without her even realizing I was certifying her services.

While we were at Starbucks, we talked about this promotional piece that was sitting on our table advertising Starbucks' music playlist. Jen asked me a bunch of questions about it, like how various elements of the promo piece were working for me, what I thought Starbucks really wanted to accomplish with it and so on. By the end, I came to a definitive conclusion about this thing all on my own: It was a piece of trash that wasn't worthy of being turned into garbage-art. (In fairness to the person who designed it, they were probably under an unreasonable deadline and their boss or client probably didn't communicate clearly what they wanted and the budget was probably way too small.)

But it was also her energy and clear love for what she does that stood out to me. It was infectious. I left our first conversation feeling like... *I want that. I want to truly enjoy what I do and to become really amazing at it.*

It would've been so easy for Jen to get stuck in her event producer job. She could've easily waited those six months to get all her ducks in a row before taking the leap. And after you've waited six months, what's waiting a couple more? And what's a couple more after that?

I've seen that movie before. I was *in* that movie before. I had one line—it was "I'll just wait until the end-of-year bonus, then I'll move on." I delivered that one-liner so convincingly it was Oscar-worthy. That turned out to be a very long movie indeed. Much longer than *Braveheart*.

Had Jen waited to take the leap, I think there's a good chance she would've suffered because of it. I know the world would've suffered because of it. Her real creativity would've been confined to the slivers of time she could find when she wasn't pouring her best hours and energy into something she didn't enjoy.

Instead, a lot more of her time was unleashed so that she could share her talents with the world. And even without the well-executed plan and the six months of savings, she found a way to make it work.

That's the possibility of leaping first.

Obviously it's easy for me to tell you to just go for it, because I'm not you, nor am I your family. But even though we may not have met yet, I believe in you. I know something you don't know about your ability to get things done when you're doing something that's authentic to you.

So do something you love.

You don't even have to "leap first." That's not really the point. Keep your day job if you like. But do something you love.

You don't have to listen to me, of course. You can listen to the voice of the Judger if you want. You can succumb to the inner resistance, the fear, the anxiety. You can listen to all of those other people who want you to play it safe.

I gathered that Jen's mother pretty much freaked out when Jen quit her job. Jen's father would've loved to see her be a math major since it turns out she's really good at that too, but that ship officially sailed by the time she hit college. She also has some brothers, one of whom would routinely send her pictures of "Help Wanted" signs. (The day we spoke it was a sign in the window of a Chipotle. I assumed he must have been being playful, but it turns out he was dead serious. Jen sighed and said, "Well, at least he's thinking about me.")

But do you *love* math? Do you *love* working at Chipotle? Do you *love* being an event producer?

Or do you *love* graphic design and studio art.

I left the question mark off because the last one was rhetorical.

I recognize it may appear as though I'm making all of this sound easy, even for Jen. But Jen was very clear with me. There was nothing easy about this.

She told me how she regularly battled with the creative person's biggest enemy and most common visitor… lack of confidence and feelings of vulnerability associated with sharing her work with other people. She told me how she regularly battled all the other forms of insecurity inherent in self-employment. With respect to moving through the fear of the leap itself, she called it "terrifying." More importantly, she told me she still felt that kind of fear about once a week.

And that's because you can't know in advance what will happen. But you knew that.

And it's because there are no guarantees everything will work out the way you want. But you knew that too.

And it's because it probably won't be totally smooth sailing for you. Nobody ever said it would be easy, not even me.

But which do you want more, something easy or something you love?

You might not get to have both. But it's your choice, it really is. So which is it going to be?

How to win an Emmy

So you want something in life. How high will you jump? How hard will you drive? How much are you willing to persevere?

Remember Tiger Woods' heyday? In 2001, he became the first player to win all four professional majors in a row. As Tiger rose in stardom, so did someone else—his caddie, Steve Williams.

I'd like to introduce you to a photographer named Ross Dettman. And let's take you back to the time Ross was sitting in this famous caddie's New Zealand home.

Ross was there on assignment for ESPN with the writer for the story, Wayne Drehs. The two were listening as Steve regaled them with various accounts of his life and career as a caddie. Steve, never short on confidence, shared success after success, and tied each of his anecdotes back to some picture or memorabilia that was sitting inside his trophy room.

There was the 1999 PGA championship flag, for example: Signed by Tiger, it said "Nice read on 17." Tiger had a long putt and thought it was to the outside of the hole, but Steve was convinced it was to the inside. Tiger trusted him. He sank the putt. If that ball hadn't gone in, things might have turned out very differently for Steve. There might never have been this interview with ESPN.

Ross and Wayne asked if they could take a peek inside the trophy room. But Steve wouldn't budge.

"Absolutely not, it's off limits to the media. Nobody has ever been in there except family and friends."

Instead, he continued with his stories. The British Open. The PGA Championship. The Masters. And again, he kept tying it back to trophies, flags, golf bags, and pictures hanging on the wall, all of which were on display in his trophy room for nobody but Steve and a select few to view.

Wayne took notes as Steve recounted his various stories. But Ross could do nothing except sit there and grow increasingly annoyed.

Finally, he couldn't take it anymore.

"Steve. You're going on and on and on about this damn room. Wayne's a writer, at least he's got something to go on. But I'm a visual guy. Every time you go on and on like that you're just killing me."

And with that, the conversation was shut down. Steve paused for what felt like an eternity. Ross figured the interview was over. The two were probably about to be ushered out.

Then Steve spoke.

"Alright then."

And just like that, Steve let the two men inside his trophy room, and Ross had 20 minutes to shoot pictures of this room that nobody in the general public had ever laid eyes on. (You can find that story, *Bag Man*, on ESPN.)

I suppose if you're on assignment shooting photos, you can take your time building trust and rapport. Or you can just take the blunt route. Ross is not the kind of guy to beat around the bush.

When Ross agreed to meet with me, I had lots of questions for him about how he made his passion a reality. After all, he has had an outstanding career. He has shot major sporting events, famous athletes and rock stars. He has been doing it for years and years.

So you can imagine I was caught off guard when his advice for people was: "You've got to be a realist. Follow your dreams, but you might fail. Have a plan B."

My idealistic heart sank a little. This coming from someone with his track record of success?

But like most things, there is always more to the story... some reason behind it, or some past secret.

So let's rewind even further—back to where things started.

Ross studied engineering at the University of Illinois at Chicago. While there, he was hungry for the quintessential college experience—you know, the one where everyone gets suited up in their gear and heads to a football game to watch their college team play a conference rival. But if that were your desire, UIC would leave you wanting.

The closest thing UIC had to that was a Division 1 hockey team that was pretty good. The problem was that nobody went to games. It's hard to get your classic college experience without cheering fans.

So Ross went hunting for an answer as to why nobody paid any attention to the hockey team. It wasn't long before he took a look at the school newspaper and happened upon his own answer. In his words, "The photos in the paper sucked." There was nothing sexy or cool about them. It was no wonder that the paper didn't entice people to venture over and check out a game.

Ross was determined to change that. So he started shooting photos of the games. He didn't have any experience other than dabbling a bit with photography in high school. But that didn't stop him.

In retrospect, his hockey photos "also sucked," but apparently they sucked less than the ones he was replacing. It wasn't too long before the school began to buy his photos and had him shoot other sports like gymnastics and baseball.

So it began. He continued working at it and honing his photography skills.

But when Ross graduated from UIC in 1986, he quickly entered adult life. He got married, and he and his wife had twins. He didn't want to be working in a cube in an office building, but the realities of his personal situation left him little choice. So he leaned on his engineering education and took his first real job out of school at a well-known architecture firm called Skidmore, Owings & Merrill.

But he kept shooting UIC sports on the side. While he was shooting at a UIC baseball game, one of the spectators asked Ross if he would shoot some pictures of his son, the third baseman. Ross said yes. This one small event turned out to be significant.

Later, that same father connected the Chicago Tribune to Ross when they were searching for a photographer to cover high school sports. The Tribune hired Ross as a freelancer. It was his first dose of serendipity.

While it seemed small at the time, whenever Ross was shooting at a game, people would consistently come up to him and ask, "Who are you shooting for?" His response was, "The Tribune." That granted him instant credibility. It became the gateway to additional assignments.

By this point, Ross wanted to pursue his photography full-time. But he didn't know how. His wife told him she was supportive if he could find a way to make enough money doing it. But he was a long way away from "enough."

So he continued shooting sports on the side while working at his new full-time job for Premisys, a software consulting firm. That meant sacrificing family time on evenings and weekends, sleeping less, and almost no time for relaxing or spending time with friends—also known as good old-fashioned hustle.

And then something happened.

A trading card company out of Milwaukee that covered minor league hockey contacted a coach from North Dakota looking for pictures of some players for their trading cards. The coach told the trading card company that the school did have pictures of the players they wanted, but that the school didn't own the rights. So he put that trading card company in touch with the person who did own the rights—Ross Dettman. More serendipity.

Looking back on that event, Ross saw it as one of the luckiest of his lucky breaks. Why?

Not everyone in that coach's shoes would have gone the extra mile to connect the company to the real owner of the images. Not everyone would have even understood that the school didn't own the rights to the photos. But because that coach was who he was and did what he did, Ross now had a relationship with a trading card company.

And in 1994, that trading card company acquired a license to do NFL photos. They offered Ross the opportunity to shoot one season of NFL and college football games. He would make a few thousand dollars for each NFL game, $700 for each college game, and he would own the rights to all of his pictures.

But Ross still had his full-time job at the software consulting company.

Maybe what happened next was pure coincidence. Maybe Ross' employers were mind readers. Maybe the universe was itching for Ross to jump headfirst into full-time photography.

Ross' employer sat him down for an unexpected heart-to-heart before he had time to contemplate the trading card offer. His employer's basic message was, "We need you to make a choice. Are you a consultant or are you a photographer?"

There was no ill will about it. The company just wanted Ross' full commitment, and they knew they weren't going to have it while he continued his aggressive after-hours freelance photography schedule. So pulling him aside and putting him on the spot seemed like the right approach to them.

Ross vividly remembers that moment he responded. There was no premeditation to it. Not even a conversation with his wife. The words just came out.

"I'm a photographer."

And that was it. A feeling of empowerment washed over him. There wasn't even any fear. It felt like destiny. *I've jumped in*, he thought to himself. *If the water is ice cold when I hit it, I'll deal with that. But I've jumped in.*

Ross went home to his wife. She was mowing the lawn at the time. He gave her the news.

"I'm done at Premisys."

The news went over like a lead balloon. Not being the risk-taking type, his wife's first reaction was, in essence, "we're doomed." Their kids were in second grade at the time. Sure, he had one season of solid income lined up. But there was no telling what would happen after that.

All of this had come completely out of nowhere for her. The NFL opportunity had materialized out of thin air. The full-time consulting job had dissolved into thin air just as spontaneously. That's a lot for anyone to take in all at once. But eventually she came around to the idea.

So Ross Dettman, part-time photographer, was going to have his shot at being all-in with his photography after all.

He began his first tour of duty shooting NFL and college football games. While he was shooting the college football games, he used the opportunity to take pictures of future stars. Later, ESPN The Magazine contacted Ross and asked to license a bunch of his college football images. And around this time, he was also hired as a freelancer by the Chicago Wolves.

So, after all of the hard work, patience and serendipity, it felt like everything was falling into place. Things were finally coming together.

Until they weren't.

The trading card company Ross worked for began to fail and pretty soon that gig evaporated. There was no more work for UIC either. And Ross had come to the conclusion that ESPN The Magazine was being "exploitative." They would tell a bunch of different photographers to show up and shoot a game, all on their own dime, but only one photo would be chosen. That meant you would spend the money to shoot a game, but your odds of having ESPN buy one of your pictures was 1 out of 8 at best. It was a losing proposition and Ross knew it.

In a short while, Ross found himself pulling in a fraction of the income he was making before. He took any freelance job he could find, but his financial situation was worsening. He was sliding into debt.

One of the freelance jobs he took during this period was for a guy who acted as a broker between photographers and trading card companies. It was an extremely unhealthy working relationship for Ross. The broker was verbally abusive and regularly tore apart Ross' work. Not only did it drain all the enjoyment out of photography for Ross, but it led to a lot of self-doubt. After two years of enduring this situation, Ross found himself on the brink of giving up on photography.

At the same time, his debt situation had come to a breaking point. Ross had thousands of dollars in credit card debt and was backed up against a wall. Completely out of options, Ross liquidated his retirement account to pay off the debt.

I can't believe I'm hedging my future to put out a fire, he thought to himself. This was like hitting financial rock bottom for him. It wasn't like he was using that retirement money for some investment for the future. He was using it to get back to "point zero." This was tough on Ross. It was even tougher on his marriage.

Now would be a good time to circle back to what I shared earlier. Remember Ross' advice to people? Here is the rest of it:

"You've got to be a realist. Follow your dreams, but you might fail. Just because you love something, it doesn't mean you'll be able to do it. Follow your dreams, but have a plan B. If you make something your profession, now you have to make money with it. There is pressure to that. You can find facets of your life competing with each other."

This is advice from a successful photographer who has been out on his own for over two decades doing something he loves. Equally so, this is advice from someone who was once on the edge of failure and watching the cracks form in the foundation of his family.

Doing what you love isn't child's play.

Many of us say we're willing to make sacrifices, but that's in the abstract. That's when we're still in a relatively comfortable spot, focusing only on the good parts of our dream, or on the bad parts of our current situation that we're seeking to escape.

Usually there is some unconscious part of us that thinks we get to have some control over what we do and don't have to sacrifice. But that's not how it works. When sacrifice comes, it comes for what it wants, not what we're prepared to give.

And when you're beaten down, and you think you might be down for the count, there is almost no amount of encouragement that will get you back up on your feet to fight some more. Quitting starts to seem like it is the only sane option left.

133

Ross got right up to that edge. He was as close as a person can get to giving up.

But maybe it was a destiny thing after all.

After some time passed, ESPN The Magazine reached back out to him. This time they were offering him legitimate assignments. Ross began shooting college football games, and with each successful assignment, he was steadily offered bigger opportunities.

One of those opportunities came in the form a phone call from someone at ESPN. They asked Ross if he would join the team responsible for shooting the Super Bowl. He tried to act calm and collected on the call, but on the inside he was like a five-year-old jumping up and down on the bed. The minute he hung up, he jumped up and down on the bed like a five-year-old.

Ross' career took an incredible turn. He went on to shoot more Super Bowls, the Stanley Cup playoffs and a string of remarkable special assignments and features.

There was *Soccer in the Storm*, the story of Bob Bradley becoming the head soccer coach of the Egyptian National Team. There was my favorite, *Unity with the Universe*, the story of a man named Tom Morgan, maker of some of the most expensive fly fishing rods in the world despite being paralyzed from the neck down.

And in 2009, Ross won a Sports Emmy for his work in *No Love Lost*, a series of stories about Chicago Cubs fans, from seven years old to over 100 years old, and their continued commitment to a team that hadn't won the World Series since 1908.

Ross' career has continued to morph and grow. While he still shoots sports, his approach has evolved. His interests have shifted too—he would prefer to shoot photos of a solo rock climber in nature over being out on the field celebrating with the winning Super Bowl team (who are "like a bunch of jackals all over a wounded gazelle...").

He has also gotten into commercial work, shooting for brands like Nike and Hammer Strength. He has been innovating with his approaches and techniques, creating truly unique and incredible output. In the evening, Ross might be capturing an image of a bloodied athlete in the heat of a competitive event. The next day, he might be staging a photo for New Balance.

Of course, none of this would have come about had Ross quit.

And he almost quit.

It happened around the time they cashed out the retirement account. At that point, when things were most difficult for his family, Ross had actually come to a decision. He was going to call off his full-time photography pursuits and go back to get a "regular job." So he went to his wife to tell her. He expected it to come as a huge relief to her.

And she said, "So now that it gets tough you're going to quit? You can't quit now."

Boom. Ross was silenced.

In his words, "If I was a fighter, she tagged me on the chin with that and I was lying on my back staring at the ceiling. It was mind-blowing. It was the most inspirational moment of my life."

At the point he was ready to throw everything away, that inspiration kept his calling alive. It's like the stars aligned. Things started to open up for Ross after that. That moment literally kicked off his career heyday.

When he looks back on his career as a professional photographer, Ross sees a series of twists of fate.

Had it not been for the father randomly asking Ross to take photos of his son playing third base, Ross would not have landed a freelance job at the Chicago Tribune.

Had it not been for the college coach referring the trading card company to Ross, he wouldn't have had the opportunity to shoot college and pro football. These photos got his foot in the door with ESPN.

Had his wife not given him the inspirational gift of her support and her no-nonsense pep-talk at his lowest point, he would have walked away from it all before things turned amazing.

To Ross, any of these events could just as easily not have happened—hence the need for a healthy dose of realism and a solid plan B. To Ross, his success was largely driven by good luck, even if he was well-prepared.

But I see things very differently.

When Ross was at Skidmore, he had a fantastic job. He was working for a prestigious firm on incredible projects. Yet something about it wasn't right. On some level, he found more meaning shooting pictures of a high school basketball game after work than he did working at the prominent architecture firm. It was so essential to him that he gave up his evenings and weekends, freelancing for five years on top of having a full-time job and having a wife and twins at home.

After that, he landed another outstanding job, this time for a software consulting company. It was a progressive firm that treated him well, paid him well, and had perks that would make many people envious. Again, something inside compelled him to give up his evenings and weekends to pursue photography on the side, and he did that for another three years.

Sure, you could look at the little breaks along the way and chalk everything up to serendipity.

But to me, I see a decade of dedication. I see someone who busted his tail nurturing his passion on the side of an insanely busy life. I see someone who honed his craft day after day and never stopped pushing himself to get better.

I see someone who ran an ultramarathon at an 800 meter pace, and then ran another one.

Have your plan B if you want it. But stick that on the shelf while you get out there and attack your plan A. Then do it again. Whatever it takes.

It's a simple recipe, really. Hustle like hell. Never give up.

Sure, you might fail. But you might do something incredible.

How bad do you want it

ere is my question to you: How bad do you want it? Whatever it is that you want. Exactly how bad do you want it? But wait. Read this first, then answer that question for yourself.

Meet Damon. He is a musician and songwriter. He majored in music in college. He got his start as a classically trained horn player (his primary instrument was the trumpet). When he finished undergrad, his intent was to go to graduate school for music performance. But to do that, he knew he needed to elevate his game when it came to his playing. He wasn't to that level yet. What that meant was that he needed a couple of years of extremely dedicated practice.

Of course there was also that pesky need to get a job.

But he knew himself well, and if he went and got a full-time job, he'd come home every day and the last thing he'd be able to do would be to practice at a high level. He needed more focus than that.

So he started architecting a work schedule around practicing his music. He took two seasonal jobs. The first was coaching youth sports for part of the year. The second was as director of a summer camp. The coaching job left him the entire morning to practice before he had to start work. The camp director job only required full-time hours in the summer and ramped down to part-time for the rest of the year.

And then there was the band. In college, Damon was part of a pop band that practiced a couple times a week and played shows on the weekend. Graduation killed the momentum with the core group of band members, so Damon grabbed the shell of the band (along with its original set of music) and rebuilt the band with some new members.

The guiding principle for his life was simple — "How am I going to make it work around my music? Because that's where my heart is."

He did all of this for a couple of years — the seasonal jobs, practicing in the mornings, and playing with the band in the evenings and on weekends.

And then something shifted.

As he put it, he found himself in a phase that looked like a rut, but it turned out to be beneficial. The truth was that he enjoyed what he was doing so much that he didn't want to give it up. He loved his seasonal jobs working with kids. He loved his band. He no longer felt the need to go to graduate school for music.

All of a sudden, this weight of pursuing grad school had been lifted, and this freed him up to pursue things in a different way. He continued working his part-time jobs and putting more of himself into the band. Over time, the band matured musically, they recorded albums and they toured.

And then they were signed by a label.

Many people think being signed by a label means you've suddenly made it as a musician. But the reality is pretty different. It's like being published as a writer. It's great — now your stuff is out there as a product and it has some distribution—but there's no guarantee it will sell.

And until it's selling, you aren't really making any money. (Even advances—which are usually smaller than people anticipate, especially for anyone new to the game—are just prepayment on potential future royalties that ultimately may or may not come). That means you still have to promote your stuff like crazy and people still have to want to buy it for you to ever financially sustain yourself with your craft.

Getting signed is the beginning of the journey, not the end.

But with this beginning, Damon began to see a new possibility. The band, the music, the thing he loved most, it had a chance at becoming a full-time, self-sustaining pursuit. No longer did it feel like making better music was the barrier standing in the way of this prospect—now it felt like the barrier was getting that music heard by people.

In music, there's really one proven way to do that. You have to play more shows.

But there were some practical problems with this.

First of all, let's talk about what "play more shows" actually means. According to Damon, it generally means playing at least a hundred shows a year—or a show about every three days—on top of practicing and any administrative work. Playing that many shows requires hitting up a lot of different cities, since you can only do so much in any given city. And playing in a lot of cities means you really don't have time to do much else.

Second of all, let's talk about the financial reality of this picture. When you're just starting out and you're somewhere between an amateur and a professional pop band, venues typically guarantee between $150 and $300 a night. Damon's band had 6 members in it. Get your calculator out and tell me if it's possible for those six people to feed themselves and pay rent on 100 shows a year at that level of guaranteed pay. (That's $15,000 to $30,000 a year, divided by 6, and that's ignoring all the other costs like gas money for your van/bus/cars.)

Obviously you hope that things start to click, the shows get bigger, the money improves, and you're making some meaningful money selling your recorded music on top of what you're bringing in from the shows. But that takes time and good fortune. The question is—for how much time can you make that situation work before you run out of money?

In a typical scenario, a band gets signed in their late teens or early twenties, before they've had time to build up much in the way of responsibilities. They can go on tour, eat street food, crash on people's floors, and get by until they get traction or they get burned out. Even then, the runway isn't usually all that long before the moment of liftoff or the moment of crash-and-burn. That's why most bands, even those with real promise, don't ever bridge the gap from amateur to sustainably pro.

But by this point, Damon's band was made up of 30-year-olds. They had 9-to-5 jobs, they were in committed relationships, and were living a so-called "regular American life." So a typical situation for them went something like this:

"Can we play in Boston next week?"

"Well, Ryan can't do it because he has a work thing he can't miss."

Game over.

Damon saw the writing on the wall. The only way his band even had a shot of going for it was if people could shed their day jobs. And the only way he could possibly get them to shed their day jobs was if he could find a way to pay them some guaranteed salary they could live on.

Here's where things get interesting.

Damon's life savings consisted of the money he was able to scrape together and set aside over the previous 10 years of stringing together his part-time work, along with some inheritance money left to him when a family member died.

Around this time, Damon and his girlfriend had made the decision not to have kids, which meant they would be two working adults with nobody to provide for other than themselves.

So as he looked at his situation and his life savings, he began to consider a radical idea:

I can hang onto this money and use it for things people usually do, like a down payment on a house and a car. Or I can invest it into turning this band into a full-time, self-sustaining business.

If you wanted to start up a business selling widgets, you would need capital. That capital would be used to make the widgets, to pay any employees and to cover your operating expenses.

If Damon wanted to turn his band into a full-time business, the formula would be the same.

First and foremost, he would have to "hire" his band members as employees as a way of buying their schedules. No more "Sorry, can't go to Boston because of [fill in the blank]…" Now they would be employees and it would be their job to go to Boston.

Second, he would be covering the costs of producing and selling the music itself (the widgets).

And third, he would be covering all of the other operating expenses (website, gas money for touring, etc.).

There was no denying it. It would be a huge risk. But this was what he loved. If he could find a way to get them across that chasm from amateur to self-sustaining professional band, it would all be worth it.

Damon decided to roll the dice.

He began taking his band members out to lunch one-on-one to pitch them on the idea. The essence of his pitch was this:

If we want to take this thing further, we have to do it now. If we wait any longer, there will be kids and commitments and people's priorities may change beyond the point of no return. We've proven to ourselves that what stands in the way for us is not 'becoming a better band' or 'making better music,' it's getting our music heard by enough people and by the right people. And we can do that, that's in our power.

Not all of them were willing to take the leap, even with some level of guaranteed income. The guitar player didn't go for it—he didn't want to risk giving up his day job. But when all was said and done, Damon had something very few bands in his situation have—a committed group of musicians who were willing to make this their one and only job, along with enough cash infused into the business to give them a little bit of runway and give the dream a real shot.

The leap of faith we have talked about is a risk for anyone. But most people's leaps do not entail taking the entirety of their life savings and using that to help support five other band members as they try to get a band off the ground. So I assumed the leap itself was probably the time Damon felt the most fear.

It turns out I was wrong.

I'll come back to that, but first, I want to share what might seem like a tangential story of Damon's around risk-taking and connecting with what's most important to you.

When Damon was first out of college and in his early days of intense practice in preparation for applying to graduate programs in music performance, he was faced with a dilemma. Damon's teacher told him that he would always be limited as a musician if he didn't make a complete change to his embouchure (which is the way musicians shape their lips and mouth on the mouthpiece of an instrument—it affects a lot of things like tone, pitch and a musician's versatility...). When Damon first learned how to play, he adopted a technique that wasn't technically correct, but he was able to get pretty awesome over the next fifteen years in spite of it. But the issue with technique was catching up with him, and he was plateauing because of it.

His teacher's basic message to him was—if you want to be a weekend warrior in a pop band, then you're fine as-is and we'll work with what you've got to make some incremental improvements to your playing. But if you want to be able to play at the next level—good enough to get into one of the best music schools, good enough to play in a symphony, good enough to break through the barriers you currently face—

then you have to start from scratch, adopt the perfect embouchure, and relearn how to play your instrument from first principles. And it may take you years to get back to the level you are at right now.

Holy cow. It reminded me of the story of when Tiger Woods was at the top of his game, winning tournament after tournament, and he took what seemed like a crazy risk to reinvent his golf swing. He was the best golfer in the world at the time. But changing his swing was the only way he could keep getting better. It was the ultimate gamble—things would have to get worse before they could get better, and there was no guarantee of ever getting back to the same level. It was the epitome of messing with the golden goose.

Damon had the same choice to make: Am I willing to move significantly backward for some unknown period of time in order to move forward?

But to answer a question like that, a person has to look many levels deeper and ask themselves things like: Why do I want this? How important is this to me, really?

Then you have to pass through that level and go even deeper, until you get all the way to The Question. There is really no other way to answer the earlier questions honestly and authentically without answering The Question, which is this:

In the end, what do I really want?

When you are up against it like this, you have to get in touch with what matters most to you. It's the only guidance you can trust.

Damon decided to make the change.

So Damon, the advanced musician—the guy who majored in music in college and performed semi-professionally for a number of years—decided to take the backwards step all the way to becoming a beginner again. He literally had to take out his old books from when he first learned to play his instrument and relearn how to play on a number of dimensions from the absolute basics. He deconstructed everything and built his playing back up block by block.

It took about four years before he reached the level he was at when he made the change. *Four years.*

I can only imagine the temptation to throw in the towel and revert back to the old way. People give up on diets after a few days. Four years!

Here's the thing. The teacher was right, and not just about the "it might take years" part, but about the other part too. After those four years, Damon broke through his previous plateau, which has even opened up the possibility of being able to play professionally at the highest level.

I took a lot away from this story. But I won't hit you over the head with it. For once, I'll let something speak for itself.

Instead, let's get back to the scariest time for Damon.

Because as you'll recall, the scariest time was not the point at which he bet his life savings on this dream. This surprised me at first, but it was because of how he viewed that bet. His primary aim was not to recoup that money. He saw it as having funded a "grant" for the band. He was ready to accept the possibility that he may never see those life savings again. The goal of the grant period was to get them through the ramp-up from amateur band to becoming a self-sustaining professional band.

So the scariest time for him was not the leap itself—it was about three months before the grant money was going to run out, right around the time Damon and I connected and he first shared his story with me. I was speaking with him when things were fresh. He was staring down the barrel of the end of the grant period, wishing the band was further along, but having to come to grips with the fact that the gamble wasn't paying off. The band wasn't making enough money to reach the holy grail of self-sustainment, and Damon could see that the growth trajectory wasn't steep enough to "get there" by the time the grant money would run out.

And to add insult to injury, the band had recently been dropped by its label, so they were back to shopping for labels and receiving none of the promotional support that a record label provides.

Barring a buzzer-beating miracle, it looked like they were going to run out of time.

Damon expressed fear about having to go back to the way things were before this amazing but brief period of pursuing the dream full-time. The fear came from those moments where the self-sabotaging voice in the head was allowed into the conversation: *Was this all just a waste of time? What did I handicap by giving up all of my savings? Look at everyone around me... they're buying houses and settling down, am I going to be fifty before that's me?*

As we sat there talking with ten seconds left on the clock for the last shot, I asked Damon if he had any regrets. Here was Damon's reply:

"Honestly, it's been worth it. Even with all those concerns. I didn't want to have to look back and think, 'Man, we were

147

so good, if only we had gone full-time, we had a chance.' Obviously I can't make people like our music. But I wanted people to be able to hear it and make their own decision. Torture for me would've been 'I wish we had tried.'"

It turns out there was no buzzer beating shot. The grant period came to an end, and some of the band members peeled off to find other jobs. Damon had to reassess his future. He explored auditioning for symphonies, which would not have been possible had he not taken four years to tear himself down to the studs and rebuild himself as a classical musician. He kicked around the concept of going back to grad school. He considered opening a studio and teaching private music lessons.

But nothing was going to stop Damon from continuing with his passion for music and performing. It didn't matter that it wasn't going to be a full-time thing for him. As he said to me, "I'm in this until the day I die."

Damon now plays with a new band that has amassed a devoted following, all while continuing with his other seasonal jobs. He has continued to put a tremendous number of hours into building his skills as a musician and is a significantly better player than he has ever been. And he continues to be one of the most satisfied-with-life people I know.

So let's come back to the original question I asked you earlier about your thing, whatever that thing may be.

How bad do you want it?

Not a lot of people are willing to put as much of themselves on the line as Damon. And I don't just mean money, either. You could substitute money with something else; it's just a symbol for whatever it is that you have to put on the line.

Not a lot of people are as in touch with their good fortune either. That was something I found so refreshing about Damon. He was the first to acknowledge his good fortune.

For example, Damon told me how fortunate he was that when he graduated from college, he didn't have to go get a full-time job like so many others. He found a way to string together part-time work. In his words, not mine: "Most people don't get that choice. They have to go into a 50 or 60 hour-per-week job and get abused. I was lucky."

He told me how much his practical reality would have been altered if he and his girlfriend had decided to have children. He quoted a statistic of it costing many parents a million dollars to raise children over the course of their lives, and how not providing for another human being significantly changes the math.

He also told me about how he was fortunate to have had the savings to give the band some runway to go for it.

I saw what he meant and could see his point that in some cases he had more financial flexibility than many people in his situation. But everyone approaches a situation with his or her own advantages and disadvantages. What stood out more to me were the choices he made given his circumstances. Lots of people have savings. Not that many use their savings to take a risk and do something remarkable.

But in the end, it's usually not about money anyway, not really. It's about something else entirely.

It's about that thing that allows a person to bet whatever they have of value on a whisper inside of them. It's about that thing that compels a person to take years of their life and risk moving backwards so they might someday be able to reach a new level. It's about that thing that allows somebody to say, come hell or high water, they'll be doing it 'til the day they die.

So what is that thing exactly? Because it's really important. Do you have it? It might be the thing that makes all the difference.

First, you have to find yourself

I'd like to introduce you to Alison Hardy. Ali is a 21st century Renaissance woman. I have lots of respect and empathy for Renaissance people. Respect might be self-explanatory. But empathy, you ask?

It goes back to something we talked about earlier. Some people have trouble figuring out one passion in life. But other people have the opposite problem. Especially 21st century Renaissance people.

This latter group tends to have spotted résumés. When viewed through the eyes of conventional wisdom, they often look like they are lost in life or are unable to focus. People tell them that nobody will hire them because their work history is too eclectic. (One of my former bosses once told me I was "unemployable" for that reason). And if these people listen to what society or their former bosses tell them, they can be made to feel as though they are defective in some way. What was once a virtue became a liability in the age of super-specialization. And I think it's a pity, because Renaissance people are awesome, and the world needs generalists just as it needs specialists.

Ali grew up in Michigan. She was a piano player from the age of four, as well as a saxophone and French horn player. In her freshman year of high school, she discovered she had a propensity for learning languages, and she became fluent in German. She went on to study foreign languages and international relations and was on the edge of settling in Germany, but met her future husband (a Brit bound for the U.S.) and decided living abroad no longer felt like the right move.

So, newly U.S.-bound herself, she became a federal IT consultant working in supply chain consulting for IBM. She also became a mother. She worked her job for seven years but realized she needed to pivot and find a job that spoke to a different side of her.

Ali made the decision to go back to school for speech pathology. After graduating, she began working in behavior analysis with a focus on autism. It was exactly the kind of job she had been dreaming of… something she could truly love.

On top of this, Ali became an artist. It began with Ali going to "wine and painting" social events with her friends and discovering she had a knack for it. The events were fun, but she also found them to be a bit uninspiring in terms of what you could paint. Around the same time, she and her husband bought a fire-damaged home. There was a picture of a rooster emblazoned on the wall, left there by the previous owners. Then, something clicked.

Ali went to work creating her first piece of original art. It's not often you get to see somebody's first piece of original art, but I was lucky enough to do just that. When she showed it to me, I was blown away. It was a magnificent painting of a rooster with brilliant colors, and I fell in love with it.

What happened next is that she shared that painting on social media and the responses were similar to my reaction. So she did a little more art and more positive feedback flooded in. And almost overnight (which are my words, chosen by comparing this to the gradual process that happens for so many others), Ali was doing commissioned artwork on the side.

Ali went from zero to making a good bit of money from her newly discovered artistic talents in less than one year. Someone once said "the internet is an amazing thing." That someone was Ali.

At the time we first spoke, Ali was working four days a week at her job in behavior analysis, a job she told me she "absolutely loves." She was also spending one full day a week doing the artwork that seemed to have fallen into her lap, which she also said she "absolutely loves." (Some of the art was for herself, and some for her growing client base.) And she was spending her remaining time with her family, rounding out a perfectly balanced life for a 21st Century Renaissance woman.

And she lived happily ever after.

The End.

But WAIT, I hear some of you say. *What about the struggle? The strife? The sacrifice? What about the gradual and grueling process of building up a portfolio, an audience, a client base? What about putting in crazy hours of stringing together multiple sources of income in the hopes that one day you can graduate from ramen noodles to rice and beans?*

Too embarrassed to admit this to Ali at the time, some of those thoughts went through my mind at first as well. It was like there was a part of me that saw it as too picture-perfect, too easy. Or that it didn't fit some preconceived notion I had of how this kind of thing progresses for a lot of people.

I bring this up because this is another thinking trap that some people can fall into—the opposite of the "overnight success" trap, where we look at alleged overnight success stories and neglect to notice the years of hard work that led up to a person's "lucky break." With this second type of trap, we become so used to hearing stories that involve lots of pain and sacrifice before the hero is victorious that we come to expect things to play out that way.

In fact, the stories I have shared until this point have more or less fit that mold. I recognize there are some risks with that. There's the risk of romanticizing the struggle, or of devaluing a person's success if they don't suffer enough for it. There's also the risk of deterring someone from going for it in their own life by focusing too much on incredible stories of hard work, struggle and sacrifice. The last thing I want to do is scare somebody from pursuing and actualizing their calling by overly-emphasizing the stories and the phases of people's journeys that contain the most difficulty.

I want to make sure I do an honest job and portray both sides. Rarely is it one way or the other… usually there is some degree of challenge, pain, sacrifice, uncertainty, you name it. Likewise, there may be the other side… things will fall into place in an almost magical way if you open yourself to that possibility.

In Ali's case, I came to see the phase of her journey following her decision to go to school, to get into behavior analysis and focus on autism, and to begin painting as an example of how wonderfully things can work out when you devote your heart to pursuing your calling.

But I also recognized I simply hadn't dug in enough to see the parts of her journey where she, too, had to slog through the mud. So allow me to back up and give you a fuller picture (according to me… it's always good to remember that).

Ali was a multi-faceted, highly talented overachiever who had a picture in her mind of what her life would look like and hundreds of pounds of expectations she placed onto herself to go along with it. She expected herself to have a big corporate job. Her parents had been in the business world and she grew up thinking of her passions as hobbies, not as something you pursue for real.

After making a radical switch away from her plan to live abroad in Germany, she landed in just that type of big corporate job she envisioned—working for IBM. She was really good at that too. And along with being really good at a big corporate consulting job came all of the trappings—like the outstanding pay (which can easily become a shiny pair of golden handcuffs) and a wonderful self-image you get to portray to your friends, your family and anyone else you meet.

The problem was that the job began crushing her soul. The hours were brutal and the travel was intense. It definitely was not a calling for her, and it even made her feel like an outright fraud at times. For years, she would express this overwhelm and emotion to her husband, and he actively encouraged her to leave: "You don't need to do this, do something you love," he would say. But for some reason, she kept with it.

But why?

The golden handcuffs may have played a role, but the real reason was tied more to self-image. Ali was proud of her self-image of being an IBMer and having this big corporate job. She was proud enough of that to put herself through a significant amount of mental anguish. Even when it wasn't working for her, she clung to it. And doing so led to a ton of self-loathing. She couldn't understand what she was doing or why she was doing it, yet in many ways she was stuck and couldn't seem to free herself. And then when she first became a mom, she was dealt another hardship—postpartum depression.

Corporate hell.

Emotional hell.

This was a dark period for her. Not only was she sapped of her creative energy, there wasn't much energy of any type. Just working a soul-sucking job followed by depression. Yay.

There was a small silver lining though. It probably went unnoticed at first. Silver linings often do. Something about this dark period triggered a change deep inside of Ali's heart. Something in her broke down. Something finally shifted.

No longer did she feel the need to fit into this idea that society placed on her, or that other people placed on her, or that she was placing on herself through her own expectations. No longer was she handcuffed by her own sense of pride. Instead, she got in touch with the Glimmer inside that led her to pursue a very different form of livelihood—one that felt meaningful and fulfilling. This was when she decided to enroll in school for speech pathology. This was the first significant domino to fall.

Even with all the pain and angst that was being caused by the trajectory she was on, it was not easy for Ali to give up her career and all of the things she had thought were so important to her. It was incredibly difficult and it took a lot of time.

During that dark period, there was a really important part of Ali that also went dark. She had completely lost her creative and artistic spark. She had no urge or energy to do anything artistic whatsoever. After 14 years of music lessons and all the years after that of playing, she didn't even have the desire to sit down and play the piano.

And this is purely my own editorial, but it takes an immense amount of psychic energy to live a life that is not authentic to you. So I am not the least bit surprised that between that and the postpartum depression, there was literally nothing left in her for the creative energy to flower.

Meeting Ali has opened my eyes to a number of things. But there is one thing her story has taught me most, and it is this:

Find yourself, and your purpose and passion will find you.

But you have to find yourself first. That's the lead domino.

Had Ali not gone through her painful process of self-discovery—almost a form of rebirth—she never would have opened the door for these amazing loves and talents to flourish.

I know there is a lot more to it than that, but I see it as the essence. And it's undeniable that things are better because of it. The world probably didn't need Ali the consultant. We're a lot better off having her art, and the work she does in autism, and I'm guessing she's a better mother because of all of this too.

Ali being a Renaissance woman, she also happens to have a black belt in dropping some wisdom on people. I share this philosophical nugget with you because it would be selfish to keep it all for myself in my own private notebook.

To all people with a calling to pursue:

"Let go of expectations. Let go of what you think everyone thinks you should be doing. Just let it go and follow that little voice inside of you. If every free minute you have you're looking at art on the internet, or you're listening to music, or whatever it is for you, that should tell you something. You have to listen to what it is that you feel passionate about. And don't worry about the money because the money will come if you're really good at something or you love something. Because that shows through in what you do."

Food for a starving artist

There is always a price to pursuing your passion.
There is always a price to not pursuing your passion.

Which of those do you think is truer? In this story, it's time to look at one of the biggest assumptions people make about doing something you love. Let me cut right to introducing you to Edward Daniels.

Edward grew up in a small town in Virginia. Anyone tagged as an intelligent kid in his hometown had a career path to follow. You became a doctor or you became a lawyer. Take your pick.

Okay, doctor it is.

So Edward shuffled off to college on the pre-med track... that is, until he got bitten by the acting bug and started questioning everything. Science just didn't seem to fit. He wasn't interested by the labs. The first thing he dissected he didn't care about one bit.

But the entertainment industry, well that was something that had never even been on his radar coming from that small town in Virginia. Yet after doing some acting in college and winning an oratory competition, he discovered that not only did he have some talent, this was a real passion of his.

So he ditched pre-med, graduated with a degree in philosophy and moved to Washington D.C. to pursue his acting passion. And almost immediately, he started picking up roles. He was doing theater and was cast in many shows including *Diamond in the Rough* at the Kennedy Center. He also picked up various television and movie roles along the way on *The District*, *Commander and Chief*, *House of Cards*, *Ladder 49*, *Step Up 2: The Streets* and many others.

Actors are usually waiting for their big break. But the statistics show that 9 out of 10 actors who commit to acting as a career don't even earn enough to support themselves, let alone become a part of the microscopic minority who "make it big." Forget your big break, can you put food on your table? Can you pay your bills?

Edward was walking the line. From an artistic perspective, he was pretty satisfied with the successes he was having. He was working a lot and being cast in great roles, so the trajectory felt good.

But he was living paycheck to paycheck in a house with a bunch of other people, he was frequently behind in rent, and the utility company shut off his power more than once because he wasn't able to keep up with the bills. Basically he was the quintessential starving artist.

Yet everywhere around him were friends of his who lived in their own apartment, or were getting married, buying homes and having children.

"When are you going to get a normal job?" his friends would ask him. It's hard for people to wrap their head around an intelligent, well-educated guy choosing to live with such financial instability in the name of what those people perceived to be some "acting fantasy."

There was a piece of Edward that even felt like he was living in a fantasy world. After you're questioned like that by the people closest to you, it's hard not to be overcome with doubt.

But just because his friends didn't understand, it didn't mean they were right, right? After all, this was his *calling*. His break would come someday, wouldn't it?

Well, a break of sorts did come. One day he was driving home and his car broke down. Stuck on the side of the road, he didn't know where to turn. So he called his mother for help.

"I'm sorry, I can't help you this time. You need to figure this out," she said. Then she hung up the phone.

There Edward was, stranded on the side of the road, unable to get home, rebuffed by his own mother. So he started calling friends until he found someone who was willing to help. And of course he had to borrow some money.

Ouch. That one left a mark.

A few months later Edward went to his hometown to visit his family for a holiday. At the end of his visit when he was saying goodbye and getting ready to get on the road back to D.C. before nightfall, his father pulled him aside.

"Your mother and I want to talk to you."

Edward knew immediately something had to be wrong since his parents never pulled him aside. And out flowed the disapproval of Edward's life decisions...

"When are you going to get a real job? We sent you to college to become a doctor and you graduate with a degree in philosophy of all things. Look at your friends and what they're doing and how successful they are."

"But I am successful," Edward said, pointing to all the shows he was booking.

"No you're not," his mom said.

Ouch. Another bruise.

A quick aside to share some thoughts...

In my many conversations with people who have pursued the road less traveled, it seems almost commonplace for people who choose to go their own way to be met with lack of acceptance and understanding somewhere along the way. But until you've actually experienced it, it can be hard to understand just how isolating that can feel. This is an aspect of that loneliness I mentioned earlier in Jon Allegretto's story. And it can be difficult to know the pain of the internal conflict this feeds... people feel caught in a catch-22. They feel like they can't win, like they're damned if they do, damned if they don't.

And I've come to see that this is often the most pivotal point in a person's journey. This is the real make-or-break moment, not some external outcome like "catching a break." Because this is where people either throw in the towel or they commit to persevering.

So back to the story, Edward left that conversation with his parents with a mix of emotions. His life didn't make sense to his parents. They clearly didn't understand him. And that was indescribably painful.

But he didn't give up in that moment. He turned it into the right kind of fuel for his journey. He came away motivated to prove to them, to his friends and to himself that this *was* what he was going to do with his life.

It's really important to be clear that this wasn't an anger-driven feeling. It wasn't a self-righteous "I'll show you!" Instead, he allowed that experience to open him to a couple of important truths.

First, he saw that it was important to him to have his parents' understanding with respect to his life choices. He realized he had to work to earn that. He could argue all he wanted, he could complain that it wasn't fair that his parents weren't blindly supportive, or he could accept the reality of his situation.

Second, he internalized the truth of their message. They were right, this was no way to live. He could no longer tolerate being a starving artist. He knew he could do better. And that meant he had to approach his life with more flexibility and be open to different ways of actualizing his aspirations.

This was a huge turning point for him. It wasn't the "big break" everyone hopes for… that magical moment that almost never actually comes when some external event frees you from your current situation and catapults you into sustained success.

This was a personal breakthrough.

At this point Edward started looking at his life through a different lens. He looked at what his friends and peers had that he wanted. He didn't do this for the sake of comparing or judging himself. He was taking an honest inventory of his life. He asked himself, "Today I can't do [fill in the blank with any one of the things he wanted], but why not?" And then an answer would come: "Because you're doing 6 theater shows a year and you're hardly getting paid for them."

This honest inventory kicked off a series of life changes, the first of which was how he divided his time. Up until this point, he hadn't really divided his time. He was aware of the fact that lots of actors have side jobs to make ends meet. But he never had interest in the cliché of waiting tables and closed himself off to it.

But he had his own Glimmer—something that he could see he hadn't paid enough attention to until this point. Edward had been hosting a karaoke night at a bar for fun. He enjoyed his experience as a DJ. Because the bar was a frequent stopping point for bachelorette parties, some of the brides-to-be would ask him if he did weddings and private events.

The more Edward considered it, the more he saw DJing as a unique opportunity in his situation. The pay was good. The flexibility of working from home and setting his own schedule offered time for him to focus on auditions. Not only that, but there was real synergy with his craft—it genuinely helped him as an actor. Every event was like a creative production, weaving together music, lights, special effects and interaction with the crowd to create a compelling experience. It provided creative juice that he could pour into acting, just like acting fed his skill as a DJ.

So Edward decided to put significant focus on building and growing a DJ business. And the more energy he poured into it, the more he was getting booked.

Edward told me the story of one wedding early on that he DJed where the bride was given golden tennis shoes as a gift, so for the first song, he had the crowd going crazy as he mixed

Footloose and Boogie Shoes together. He loved the notion that he may have helped create a memory that the bride and her family would remember for years to come.

After the event he received positive reviews, giving him further conviction he was on the right path. And positive reviews from experiences like that turned into referrals and more opportunities.

As Edward shifted a portion of his energy toward DJing, he also shifted his focus with respect to the acting opportunities he pursued. The simple fact was that film acting was much more lucrative than theater. One day on a television or movie set provided the financial equivalent of one week of doing theater. So Edward began turning down many theater opportunities in favor of film, and he became more selective in the film and theater opportunities he pursued in general.

The next big shift came when he recognized his own failure to properly value himself as an actor and place a corresponding level of expectations on how much he should earn for doing a gig.

Edward described this to me as a common trap that actors fall into; they don't properly value themselves. He explained how as an actor, you're constantly chasing jobs and experiencing rejection more than success. When you do land a role, it's easy to convince yourself that you are lucky to have any role at all, even if the pay is crappy and the perks are non-existent.

For the new Edward, there would be no more "Okay, I'll do seventy-five-dollar-a-day background work." Making two or three dollars an hour for upwards of 20 hours? Not a chance.

Instead, his approach became, "What am I getting paid per gig? What am I charging? What does the contract look like?" He wouldn't take an acting job if it didn't meet his financial standards or meaningfully progress him in his career. He raised his DJ rates to align with the local market and the true value he was providing.

Changing his sights from "getting by" to "thriving" made a huge difference in Edward's life. There was an immediate shift in the growth of his roles, his business and his personal fulfillment.

When I met with Edward and he agreed to have me share his story, I came to see that part of his motivation came down to two things.

First, just like me, he is also an enormous advocate of pursuing passion and purpose in life. He is a living example of somebody who has chosen to go his own way, even when it was counter to all the pressures of society, friends and family. And when we spoke, he enthusiastically rattled off similar examples, like Compass Coffee in Washington D.C. which was started by two ex-Marines who knew nothing about coffee but managed to bring an incredibly authentic local business to life. He told me about another guy he knew who opened a late night snack delivery business in a college town. He told me about a woman he knew who "took her one little story global" by headlining her own one-woman show. I could tell he was visibly lit up by these stories.

The other reason I think Edward was so willing to share brings us all the way back to where I started this story.

There is always a price to pursuing your passion.

I, like many others, have often focused on the sacrifices one needs to be prepared to make when pursuing a dream or a calling. I never used to see the "starving artist" notion as a problem.

But Edward hates the term "starving artist." He sees it as legitimizing the idea of being broke in the name of your passion, which doesn't have to be the case. It may be a romantic notion to be willing to sacrifice so much to follow an inner calling, but it fosters limiting beliefs.

As Edward shared more about his perspective, he told me this about the acting community:

"There are things we do in our twenties that result in us being a starving artist in our forties."

To illustrate, he recalled a time a friend said something he never forgot: "Sure you're doing shows and you're getting good roles, but at the end of it, what do you have to show for all of this?"

Those words sunk in deeply. At the time, Edward was living in a house with a group of random people. A committed relationship had recently come to an end and he realized after the breakup, "I literally can't make it on my own." He had no sense of freedom. It was a miserable feeling for him.

Maybe it was because of his friend's potent words, maybe it was because of his parents' penetrating message, or maybe it was because of his own internal drive and aspirations. Most likely it was a combination of all three. But Edward made a deliberate change in his life: He went from being financially unstable and accepting that as the reality of pursuing an acting career to systematically overhauling his life so he could pursue his passion and afford a lifestyle he deserved.

Today, Edward has taken those hard-earned lessons and uses them to coach actors on his practical philosophy of living the *artist life* on your terms. He described it to me as follows:

"Figure out the salary you need. Broaden your available opportunities by getting your portfolio in the hands of every casting agency. Register in other cities. When an opportunity comes, you should negotiate just like it's a normal job. You should understand the time commitment, the pay and any other details and determine if it meets your financial expectations and if it can be used to progress your career. Don't fall into the trap of the 'I'm in it for the experience or exposure' mindset. Too many artists adopt an unspoken belief that, 'Well, I'm an artist, at some point in the future the value I provide will be acknowledged financially.'"

But more generally, he gives advice that applies to anyone pursuing their calling. He used this advice to transform his life and make his entertainment career a sustainable reality. This is what he shared:

"Make a plan and get it on paper… 'This is what I want over the next year of my life and here are the little steps that get me there.' You don't have to lose 100 pounds in the next month. You just have to begin. I make a lot of lists… in my opinion, list are so simple. They are just moments of setting your goals on paper and checking them off. Plot it out and let that motivate you to make it happen. And surround yourself with people who are doing it and are successful so you can ask what they are doing and how they are making it work."

So coming full circle, yes… there may be a price to pay when pursuing a passion. But according to Edward, that price doesn't have to be anything close to signing up for financial distress.

How about the other statement?

There is always a price to not pursuing your passion.

This is the aspect of Edward's story that resonates with me on the deepest level. It comes back to the essential reason I am writing and sharing this book.

Ultimately, pursuing your calling is about being yourself. Edward is an example of someone who never gave up on being himself.

Even as he struggled to make ends meet, even when he felt like he was letting his parents down or like he was letting himself down, he still knew he had to find a way to make this life work. Time and time again, he chose authenticity over caving into external pressures. He persevered and followed what was true to him.

I want to illustrate what can happen when you do this by telling you a couple of brief stories that Edward shared with me.

In the early days of acting, Edward described a time when he would see other actors and he felt the pull to change his style to be more like them. He felt something similar before his DJ gigs, where he would think to himself: "What am I going to do, what am I going to wear…" In essence, he felt he needed to be somebody in particular that would win over other people.

But he didn't cave into that urge because on a deeper level, he knew it didn't feel right.

And over time, he saw his DJ clients coming back to him saying, "We love you, we love your voice, the crowd just responds differently when it's *you*." Likewise, he was securing acting roles in just the same way.

In his words, he began brushing away the idea of having to be "the thing that's not quite you."

I felt chills when he spoke those words. I think we've all felt that before. We have all compromised at some point and have been the thing that is not quite ourselves. It never feels right. I can say without a speck of doubt that it's not the way to a deep sense of fulfillment and contentment in life.

Edward recounted a time when he was in a relationship with someone whose friends were all in accounting, law and government. Every time he went out, he dreaded the common cocktail party question, "So what do you do?" If he told them, "I'm an actor and a DJ," he felt like he squelched the conversation. He felt awkward. So he started editing himself.

But one day when he was at an event, the question came up and he didn't want to edit anymore.

"I'm an actor," he said with confidence.

Then another guy turned around and said, "Hey, didn't I see you in *Rent*? You were amazing!"

It was a moment of self-realization for Edward. It was like the universe was showing him *you don't need to be ashamed. Just be you.*

The universe took it a step further as well. The day came for Edward's mother to watch him perform in that very same show for the first time. She came up to him after the show with tears in her eyes. He could tell by the look on her face that she finally saw who he was and understood how happy it made him to be doing his thing.

From those points on, Edward was able to let loose and discover a new confidence, a new sense of self-worth and a new sense of freedom—not because he had other people's approval, but because he shed the inauthenticity once and for all and discovered the joy and fulfillment that comes with doing so.

More than any other lesson I have taken from Edward, it's this that has influenced me the most. Despite the immense external pressure that was consistently trying to push Edward down other paths that didn't feel like they were *him*, he managed to hold onto what he knew to be true for himself the entire way. And by pursuing his truth, he grew to become even more authentic and free.

My story

I have been a working adult for many years, but I am in the early stages of pursuing a calling. Such is the case for a person who learns about himself slowly. That is why so much of the story I am about to share takes place before my leap of faith.

I grew up in a middle class family of four in upstate New York. As a child, I was fortunate that school came easily to me. I had a wide variety of interests in and out of school. I was strongest in science and math, but tended to enjoy other subjects more. I was decent in the sports I played, but I lacked the competitive fire one needs to have to be really good. I loved most of the activities I pursued and often had trouble choosing how to allocate my time. But if forced to choose, music was my deepest passion throughout my early years.

When it came time to head to college, I considered going to school for music. But my parents warned me that the life of a musician wasn't an easy one, and that doing it for money could spoil my love for it. It seemed like reasonable advice, and I didn't want to risk losing a love like that, so I pointed myself in the direction of the academic subjects I was strongest in—science and math—and applied to an engineering school. I didn't even really understand what engineers did at the time. But my parents told me I would have no trouble getting a great job. I didn't have any better ideas, so I went along with it.

After my freshman year at the University of Virginia, it was clear to me that engineering wasn't my thing. My parents encouraged me to stick it out. They told me I didn't have to be an engineer, but that the engineering degree was well-respected in the working world and it would be something I could always fall back on. The prospect of switching majors also daunted me because it meant I would have to take a step backwards.

So I decided to stick it out on the engineering track and I chose the least challenging of the engineering programs at my school so that I'd have a tiny bit of space in my schedule to take other coursework I was more interested in. Considering I only had a year invested by that point and some of my completed coursework would have translated if I had switched majors, I can only smile at the naiveté of that younger me who had contemplated that decision when he came to the crossroads.

At the end of my sophomore year, I wanted to spend the summer in my college town. I needed to find a job quickly if I had any hope of affording rent, and I stumbled upon an opening in a graduate school biomedical engineering research lab. I applied the moment I discovered the position and rejoiced when I learned a few days later that I had secured the job. This all seemed like an innocent decision at the time, but that choice ended up altering the course of my life—something I only recognized in hindsight.

One day, while talking to one of the graduate students in the lab, he asked if I knew about the fifth year master's degree program that the school offered. I knew nothing about it.

"It's a master's degree in one year. The school pays for it. Even if you don't end up using it, it's only one year and it's free. It's a no-brainer," he said.

I respected this guy and it felt like I was being let in on some secret stock tip that was too good to pass up. I enrolled in the program.

As I continued with school, I had just enough interest in the classes I took to keep me going. But I wasn't gaining clarity about what to do after graduation, probably because all my time was going toward a demanding curriculum that was only of moderate interest to me. I hadn't exactly spent much time exposing myself to other possible avenues, in part because my space for electives had been filled with graduate coursework. By the time I had entered my fifth and final year and I was running out of time to figure things out, I was as lost as ever about what to do next.

Without a clear notion, I found myself continuing down the path of least resistance—extending my life as a career student and moving to Boston to begin a Ph.D. program. Again, the downside seemed low. School was paid for by a research grant and I was given a stipend of $20,000. It was effectively a low-paying job that compensated you with Ph.D. credentials. I rationalized that I might enjoy teaching as a college professor. Taken together, it seemed plausible enough to give it a go.

But a year into the Ph.D. program, after I finished the coursework and had nothing left but a four-year research project and dissertation to complete, I began to feel that the cracks in my rationale were becoming exposed. The problem came to a head when I realized three things:

1. Most of being a professor in the field I was studying was actually about lab research.
2. I hated doing lab research.
3. I liked the idea of teaching college, but not in the subject I was getting a degree in.

These realizations led me to my first existential crisis at the ripe old age of 24. I was clearly on the wrong path. This existential crisis also coincided with my two-month process of studying for the Ph.D. qualifiers—the most intense exam of my life—which required me to teach myself thermodynamics from scratch since I had never taken that prerequisite as an undergrad.

I began having zaps of shooting chest pain at random points throughout the day. A quick search on the trusty worldwide web led me to the conclusion that I most certainly had an undiagnosed heart condition, and that I needed to see a cardiologist ASAP.

I found one. First, they ran several tests in their office which turned up nothing. Next they sent me home with a bunch of electrodes taped to me and a monitoring device hanging from my belt with a button. Every time I was stabbed in the chest, I was to retaliate by pushing the button, which would log that exact moment in time to allow the physicians to go back and get a reading on what was going on inside me.

A couple of days later they had analyzed the data and they delivered the news: There was nothing wrong with my heart.

They told me it was most likely a case of heart palpitations, a non-painful condition for which Web M.D.'s descriptions did not match my symptoms. But since the witchcraft and wizardry of modern medicine had historically sent me home dissatisfied without any concrete answers, I formed my own conclusion: Spirit guides must have been trying to send me a message that I needed to drop out of grad school and get out of town, stat!

"Whoa whoa whoa, spirit guides, I'm not ready for that. Shouldn't I just pass the qualifiers first in case I change my mind and ever want to finish my Ph.D.?"

ZAP! I keeled over in pain.

"Okay, okay, I get it! I'll listen!"

I didn't though. I was trying to pull a fast one on the spirit guides. I kept studying. I studied and studied and studied. And I actually passed those crazy qualifiers, a modern day miracle.

ZAP!

"Okay, okay," I bargained with the angry spirit guides, "I get it! I'll drop out already."

But I was too much of wuss to completely drop out, so I asked for a year off in case I changed my mind. Thankfully the heart zapping stopped, which empirically proved my spirit guide theory. But I never went back to school to finish my dissertation.

Instead, I went searching for a "regular job." I was tired of school, where one always has something hanging over one's head that one "should" be doing when one isn't studying or making progress on one's thesis. I thought to myself, *wouldn't it be nice to just go to work and then turn off my computer, go home and enjoy my life?*

What a sweet, naïve boy I was.

I applied for jobs and found my first job out of school at a small strategy and management consulting firm. It was clearly a business job for which I had zero relevant experience, but I finagled my way into it because they focused on consulting to medical device, biotech and pharmaceutical companies and valued my master's degree in biomedical engineering.

My fantasy of turning off my computer at the end of the day, going home and enjoying life did not come true. The next year and a half were a wild ride. Rather than regale you with all of it, I'll share one story that encapsulates the reason it only lasted a year and a half.

I was sitting at a conference table with my manager and the partners at a ridiculous hour of night. We were on the phone with a potential client we were pitching who was headquartered in Japan. The translator on the other end of the phone asked a question in slightly broken English.

"How many project… sales territory optimization project specifically… have your team led as company?"

I remember scrambling to think about how I could answer *zero* without actually saying the word *zero* or any of its synonyms. I went to speak up but my boss held his hand across my chest to stop me.

"Many," my boss interjected. "We have led *many* sales force optimization projects for large pharmaceutical and medical device companies."

This was, of course, not true. Yet we always happened to have the perfect experience profile for every client's highly specific need.

My boss then handed the call over to me to take them through our pitch deck, muted the phone, and told me to "Go slowwww…" before unmuting the phone and waving me on.

I remember my brain running off to places you don't want your brain going when you need your wits about you. I imagined myself yelling "How do you say 'I QUIT' in Japanese?!" and then tearing the tie off my neck, wrapping it around my forehead, kicking down the conference room door and running off cackling with glee like the maniacal shell of a human I had become.

But I did not. I could not. I had bills to pay. I had a lease on an expensive apartment in the city. Plus my rent had effectively doubled after my recent breakup left me without a "roommate." I had no backup job lined up… who has time to look for one of those when you're working 14 hour days? I had no savings… I was only a couple of years out of school and had more debt than the U.S. government. I was stuck.

So I did what I felt I had to do in that moment. I faked my way through the 15-page PowerPoint presentation—which was full of maps of Japan we had pulled off the internet that very well could have been from the 1990s—and I escaped without being discovered as the underpaid fraud I had become.

The client agreed to sign on with us. I felt terrible about myself. My boss patted me on the shoulder for a job well done and handed me my reward—another impossible deadline and an assignment to read a book on Japanese business culture over the weekend so I didn't make any American businessman mistakes on my upcoming trip to Japan.

Except I never did make it to Japan. I remained an indentured servant for only a few more days before I realized I couldn't do it anymore.

I walked into the office in jeans, a t-shirt and flip flops and headed past the cubicle farm of my fellow slaves who sat typing away in their suits and ties as I made my way to the executive offices. I remember the slaves whispering amongst themselves. They sensed a rebellion.

I knocked on the boss's door and went to tell him I was resigning. Before I could speak, he said, "Let me guess, you're quitting."

"Yes," I said.

"Well you can't quit, we're firing you first," he said.

In a flash, my brain flooded with memories of all the times the company had broken the news to us about someone else they had allegedly "let go." It was like watching the end of *The Usual Suspects* as my brain connected all the dots from the past two years in rapid succession.

A-ha! Those people hadn't all been let go! They tried to quit but the story the rest of us were told was a tactic the company used to preserve their puffed-up egos and keep the cultish narrative from being discovered!

When I left that day, I was angry. But at the same time, I was free! At last, it was my time to ride off into the sunset in the direction of career paradise. I made a list of all of the things I would never, ever do again for as long as I lived:

Never again will I allow myself to be swept up into tremendous stress resulting from what is ultimately a manufactured sense of urgency. Never again will I do work that runs counter to my personality or violates my core values as a human being. Never again will I allow myself to become stuck as a slave to the almighty dollar doing work I do not enjoy.

I figured it wasn't possible for me to make a mistake like that again. There had been too much pain, too much stress and too much learning that would stay with me for a lifetime. Of course that, too, proved to be naïve.

After quitting and simultaneously being fired, an honor bestowed upon very few people, I set out looking for something totally different to pursue. But I was still as lost as ever. And I didn't have enough savings to dilly dally. I needed to figure out my next step quickly.

I remember feeling drawn to writing, but that wasn't something I felt was prudent to count on to pay the bills. So I started thinking about jobs I might enjoy that would also afford me enough time on the side to write.

I remembered back to the days when I thought I might want to teach. I didn't have the credentials to be a college professor, but a thought crossed my mind. *What about teaching high school or middle school?*

The mission was something I could get behind. And summers off would give me time to write. So I decided to go for it. Although I didn't have a degree in teaching, there was enough of a shortage of teachers in math and science (especially in rougher schools) that I was able to snag a job.

Sadly, I didn't last a year as a high school teacher. I came away with a deep respect for high school teachers and what they do, and complete clarity that it wasn't for me. While I liked the mission, I was terrible at the discipline and classroom management side of things. And I couldn't hack being "on stage" all day long. I'm an introvert. Introverts like me need to be frequently watered with silence and alone time or we wither and die.

I don't consider my first consulting job or my teaching stint to be mistakes on my path. They were necessary erring/wandering, especially for a person who got a late start to contemplating possible paths in life. I probably could not have figured out if they were a fit any other way than by giving them a try. And I learned about myself from those trials. Plus I had ruled something out.

Now it's great to rule something out, but in a world where the possibilities are nearly infinite, eliminating one or two of those possibilities tends not to be enough to set you on a clear and direct path to vocational bliss.

And I still didn't have enough savings to take any real time off so that I could step back and contemplate my situation. Instead, I rushed into another job to keep myself afloat.

This time I followed some of my former consulting colleagues to a different consulting firm, one that I was assured bore no resemblance to the first one in terms of its values or its degree of stability. I signed on to work remotely for them as a contractor, which gave me the flexibility to live in North Carolina and escape the northern winters.

My first several months with the company were an immense relief from the prior months of waking up at 5 a.m. to ensure I was on time for the moment when my high school students would start lobbing chairs out of second story windows. Because I worked from home ninety percent of the time, I would roll out of bed minutes before my first meeting.

With no commute and the ability to do chores like laundry while I sat as a listener on conference calls, I was blown away by the wonders of this new luxury I had never before experienced in my life: *free time*.

"But what on God's green earth do I do with this 'free time' you speak of?" I would ask wise people who were more familiar with the concept than me.

"Take up a hobby," they would tell me. "Learn to cook. Learn to golf. Learn to crochet."

So I did. I began cooking and experimented with new diets. Without meaning to, I lost 20 pounds and discovered the secret to boundless energy that I would one day forget.

But more importantly, I finally turned to the writing I had aspired to do. Each day, when I was done with work, I would chip away at my first novel. And for the first time in my life, I finished a manuscript. I submitted it for publication. I got a little bit of interest, but nobody bit. The feedback was that it needed a lot of rework, and by that point I was tired of that project and ready to move onto the next one.

The other thing that happened during this time is that I became drawn to the idea of starting a small business. I began using some of my free time to work on coming up with business concepts. I bought *Small Business for Dummies*, a book that would come along for many moves halfway across the country and sit on my shelf collecting dust for lots of years.

For about a year in my new job, things went well. I was good at my job and it was laid back enough that I was able to pursue passion projects on the side.

But I couldn't shake the nagging itch in the back of my mind that the day would come when things would change.

Either the good times wouldn't be so good anymore, or else I would need to honor this desire I felt inside to pursue work that was more meaningful to me.

That intuition proved to be right. One day, my boss called me on the phone.

"Mike, we need you to relocate and join us at our headquarters. We're prepared to offer you a substantial raise to encourage you to say yes."

I was immediately overcome by incredible inner conflict. I had just moved to North Carolina. I loved the lifestyle and my cost of living was low. I had recently gotten engaged and bought a house. I didn't want to have to give any of that up to move back to Boston.

But I wasn't given the option to continue as-is, so I was either in or I was out.

I remember the inner conflict like it was yesterday. On one shoulder, I had a voice telling me that I was happy, I loved my new home and my new hometown, and that I could just find another job in the area. On the other shoulder, I had a voice that told me I couldn't pass up the assurance that came with this raise and the fact that I was rising in this company. That voice even convinced me that if I stayed the course, I might be able to retire early.

In fact, I took that idea and ran with it, building a spreadsheet to see how quickly I might be able to retire if I made the amount of money they promised and lived as conservatively as possible. Microsoft Excel revealed that it was conceivable for me to retire in ten years. I saved the file and named it "10 Year Plan."

I called everyone I knew including one of my best friends, Nate. I always listened to Nate; he was a voice of reason.

"I could retire super early," I told Nate.

"You really think you'll work there that long anyway? Or that your lifestyle won't expand? Besides, money doesn't buy happiness, dude."

"But retirement does…" I said.

"If you say so," he said. I could almost hear the eye roll on the other end of the phone.

I knew Nate was right. Making decisions because of money never seemed to work out very well for people. But the pull was too strong. Somewhere along the way, the desire for financial security was programmed into me in a deep enough way that I had become its slave. My fiancée and I had a lot of student loan debt, and I desperately wanted to get out from underneath it.

So a few weeks later, my fiancée and I were driving up the coast in a moving truck with all of our worldly possessions in the back. I had signed on as a permanent employee.

It didn't take long for things to take a turn for the worse. Within three months of arriving, the workload at the company spiked, my stress level sky-rocketed and my heart sank to the depths of the earth.

At that point, I learned firsthand some indicators that it may be time to leave your job:

- When Sundays are ruined by the Sunday Blues, a mental health condition where an otherwise nice weekend day is spoiled by rampant anxiety and dread about going back to work on Monday.

184

- When you wake up on weekdays feeling good for two or three seconds until your brain pieces together who and where you are, then rips the good feelings out of your heart, throws them on the floor and invites the cast of Riverdance in to trample them with an Irish jig. (The first few seconds after waking can be a strange time, no?)
- When your nights are plagued by arguments with work people in your dreams, or in your insomniac daydreams.
- When you wake up to a damp pillow and realize, *that's not drool… those are tears.*
- When you divulge to random strangers that you don't like your job, when all they really wanted to do was pay for their groceries in peace and go home.

I suffered from all of these and more. And there wasn't even close to enough time to pick up crocheting. I finally reached my breaking point. I gave them my notice.

With no job and no idea what was next, I once again found myself moving halfway across the country with a limited safety net of short term savings, mounds of student loan debt and a need to figure out what was next for me as quickly as possible. The motivation behind this move was to settle near my wife's hometown outside of Chicago after having recently gotten married.

We moved in with my wife's parents while we looked for a place of our own and while I started applying for jobs. I gave myself two months for a "sabbatical" where I could explore new potential career paths. But days after that proclamation to myself, I fielded an incoming call from the company I had just left.

"I know you don't really want to be a consultant forever and this was just a way for you to make money while you figured things out," my former boss began. "But while you're figuring out your next step, how about working remotely on a project basis as a contractor for me?"

This doesn't seem like a good idea, the voice within warned. Perhaps it was a test from the spirit guides.

"Sure," I heard myself say, realizing spirit guides were no match for that scared child within who was utterly enslaved by this fear of financial instability.

Just as the voice had warned, project worked turned into more project work, which turned into full-time work and eventually turned into me helping the company open up a new office in my new city. I felt like the monkey in the cage who keeps pressing the lever no matter how many times he gets shocked. My sabbatical hadn't even started and I had already abandoned all of my job searching efforts, my creative projects, my business ideas and my self-esteem, and I was back on the path I knew in my heart of hearts was not my calling.

The spirit guides must have been shaking their heads with disgust. Or maybe spirit guides don't have heads, I'm not sure.

Within a couple of months, the familiar sense of dread returned. While I still didn't know what I wanted to do with my life, I knew consulting to large corporations wasn't what I was put on this planet to do.

This feeling of being out of place was amplified by meeting so many people through my project work who were clinging desperately to their jobs even though they seemed utterly dissatisfied. The starkest examples were the CEOs who were making ten million dollars a year but were clearly unhappy. I figured yachts must be just a little too enticing to give up, and yacht parties can't be cheap.

But what hit closer to home were all of these mid-level managers and employees who clearly seemed dissatisfied and lacked a sense of purpose. Yet they, too, were desperately clinging to their jobs, not because they had yachts to maintain, but because they had a mortgage, or kids in college, or they just liked to take vacations and golf on the weekends and afford organic food.

None of it sat well and I felt another existential crisis brewing. I desperately wanted to shut my existential crisis brewery down and stop all of those bubbly bottles of misery from escaping. And I'd love to tell you that the next day I grabbed an empty printer paper box, packed up my picture frames and my desk plant and the company's stapler and ran for the hills.

But if I told you that, I'd be lying.

We didn't have a yacht to maintain at our household, nor were we buying organic at the time… we were slowly being poisoned by Monsanto products and rolling the dice with GMOs. But we did have a boatload of student loans. And we had two fourteen-year-old cars that were on the edge of crapping out, which could have made us late to our golf game if we were golfers, which we were not. And we were saving up for a down payment on a home.

So, "If I can just get to the end-of-year bonus…" became my theme song.

Then the bonus would come and go and the cycle would repeat again. My depression deepened. I felt like a slave. I read Thoreau's *Walden* and fantasized about a simple life off the grid. But no matter how many times he shouted at me, "Get your free papers!" and no matter how many shows I watched about tiny houses, I remained a slave.

I'm embarrassed to admit it, but this went on for years. It wasn't until I became a dad that things shifted. Every week I would travel for work and by the time I came home, something about my son had changed.

"My God," I would say, "he chucked that sweet potato puree farther than he's ever chucked it before. When did he start doing that? That boy might be a major league pitcher."

One day when he was 9 months old, I was randomly at home for a week of no travel. That day, that little guy took his first steps. I didn't miss it! But I could have. It was the luck of the draw. That was my tipping point.

I had spent over seven years with that company before I pulled the rip cord. It's worth mentioning an important financial detail about my life. Remember my 10 Year Plan spreadsheet? Well contrary to what it had forecasted many years earlier, I was not a mere two or three years away from retirement bliss. According to the spreadsheet, my absolute best case scenario if we cut way back and lived as conservatively as possible was that I had a minimum of… drumroll… ten more years before I could retire. True story.

Had I underestimated the cost of living difference between the cities I lived in? Had I messed up other assumptions? Had

I inputted a formula error? Should I have renamed it the "2 Year Plan" to see if that made a difference? Spreadsheets: Garbage in, garbage out. Another important life lesson.

Where I landed next was working for a corporation that manufactured fitness equipment. I genuinely enjoy fitness and became certified to coach fitness on the side as well, so it was refreshing to have a real interest in the industry I was in and the content of my job. I also really loved the people I was working with and felt a connection with many of them.

But the company suffered from more than its fair share of Corporate America shenanigans. The hours and stress levels were not healthy. The instability of the company was unsettling. The company went through several CEOs in a few short years. I was put under a different boss every year. And I had a front row seat to decisions at the top that quite literally drove me insane because they were so obviously bad for the company.

I wish I could tell you that as soon as I saw the trajectory, I listened to my heart and followed the advice I have shared thus far in this book. But by now you've picked up on the pattern. I stayed the course. A part of me kept hoping things would improve at the company; instead, the situation worsened. I was offered several promotions along the way and said yes to them all, even when the voice inside warned me about the added stress I was taking on and the more deeply entrenched I was allowing myself to become. I rose to the senior executive ranks, all the while plainly seeing the toll it was taking on me mentally, emotionally and physically. Maybe under different circumstances things would have been okay, but certainly not at this time in this company. Things were too wild, too movie-like and too unhealthy.

On one level, this period was doing its inner surgery on me below the surface of my conscious awareness.

As I watched the company being mismanaged by its leaders as they made terrible decisions, there were people around me who were able to brush it off and chalk it up to that just being how things are in wacky old Corporate America. I came to see I was fundamentally different from those people.

As I witnessed incredible shenanigans and unfathomable levels of corporate B.S., there were people around me who largely ignored it, seemingly able to roll their eyes and go on about their day. I came to see I was fundamentally different from those people.

And as I went to work for a prolonged period where I realized my professional life had degenerated into slogging it out to collect a paycheck, there were people around me who seemed to be comfortable doing the same thing and living for whatever satisfaction they could milk from their nights and weekends. I came to see I was fundamentally different from those people.

While it should not need to take a person over a decade to learn certain things about himself, this seemed to be what finally drove these points through my very, very thick skull. This was the point at which I began seeking inspiration from the people whose stories I shared with you.

It's difficult to describe how much of a relief it was to find people who spoke my language and who valued many of the same things I valued. They talked about the importance of pursuing a calling. They shared how they could never find satisfaction slogging it out just to collect paycheck. They weren't prepared to have their destiny controlled by the whims of leaders who made terrible decisions, nor by the strange set of values propagated by the overwhelming majority of corporations today. They could not fathom following a safe and more traditional route in life if it meant they would have to ignore the call of their hearts.

Just to know that others felt the way I did was enough to fill me with a sense of relief, validation, inspiration and motivation.

I brought them the questions I had been wrestling with for many years by this point. *How important is it to love what you do for work? Should you pursue your passion as your career? When should you go for it? When is it better to keep your hobby as a hobby? When should you go all in and risk everything or nurture it on the side?*

Beyond these questions, I was also trying to understand what it was about me that was preventing me from being able to figure things out in my own life. Was it simply because I lacked clarity? Did I lack clarity because of my late start in life on this reflection? Was it because I had too many passions? Was it a dearth of conviction? Was it because my expectations were too high? Was it because all of the things that give me a sense of purpose tend to be difficult to rely on for income? Was it a lack of patience or a lack of follow-through? Was it because I had a family to support and it felt too selfish to risk putting them through any instability? Was it a lack of courage and willingness to take a risk?

Living in this "land of opportunity," it has been instilled in me from very early on just how lucky I am. Not only am I not going hungry, but I am blessed to have a choice when it comes to my livelihood. Not everyone does. Many people are born to different circumstances. Sometimes one can't help but feel a little guilty about having a desire to pursue more meaningful work, even though it truly isn't a selfish pursuit to follow a calling. Those feelings arise nonetheless, because even in a land of opportunity, there are a ton of people who have to work very sub-optimal jobs, and often for abysmal wages.

But by this point, where had that gift of choice gotten me? Usually it had put me in situations where I had a "great job," but something felt missing and I felt drawn to finding a different livelihood that aligned more with a sense of purpose. And then I would beat myself up for not feeling more grateful for this job that so many people would be lucky to have. That was the loop, and it had been playing out for well over a decade.

As I connected with all of those people, they showed me that I wasn't crazy. They, too, had felt the profound discomfort of doing something that missed the mark for them. I think everyone has had that feeling… something inside of us says, "This feels off." It can show up as a sense of lack or a feeling that something is missing. It can be subtle, or it can be obvious and painful.

My strong view—which has only grown in strength because of my various missteps and because of my connections with these people—is that this feeling is a clear indicator that you should be doing something else, not out of

192

your own self-interest, but for other reasons entirely. It's like a message from the universe that something is out of alignment.

Out of alignment hurts. That is life's way of nudging you to get back in alignment with the real you. But when you're living in a way that aligns with the real you, you discover an incredible inner reservoir of strength that is born from true joy, contentment and living with a sense of purpose. You tap into a force that is much more powerful than the force that usually governs our lives—our ordinary desires and our personal will. Ordinary desires and personal will aren't powerful enough forces to help a person overcome the challenges and stay committed over the long haul.

How else would Ross have been able to shoot photography for 10 years as a side job on top of working a full-time job with twins at home? How else would Jon have demonstrated a similar level of hustle for so long? How else would Jen have been able to overcome her frequent encounters with fear and uncertainty? How else would Damon have been able to summon the courage to put every last dollar he had into sharing his music with the world, or to take years of his life to move backward in his music ability so that someday he could reach new levels? How else would Ali have found her way through her dark period and manifest her amazing new life? How else would Edward have overcome the consistent rejection from friends and family and stay so true to himself?

And how else would just about every person I talked to have stumbled into a unique combination of professions that allowed each of them to financially provide for themselves while pursuing their soul's craft?

Personal will couldn't have accomplished one-tenth of that. We find strength like this from being authentic and true to ourselves. We listen to the still, small voice inside that impels us to pursue our unique path. It doesn't matter if someone chooses to do that on a full-time basis or pursues it on the side. It doesn't matter if it's met with wild cheers of approval or it's lost in relative obscurity. It's not about the outcome. It really is about being completely authentic and true to yourself and having the courage to give those gifts to the world.

I came away from this period of exploration knowing beyond the shadow of a doubt that I needed a radical change in my life. But I was still my family's sole source of income, so I had to find a way to do it without upheaval on the home front.

I began waking up every morning at 4 a.m. to carve out meaningful time for self-discovery and to get back into writing. At this point in my journey, I did follow my own advice. I meditated, journaled and spent lots of time with the questions for reflection, and I supplemented all of this with some of the other approaches I shared with you as well. I believe in those recommendations because they worked for me. For the first time in my life, I began to gain a sense of clarity about the direction I wanted my life to head in.

Then came a twist I wasn't expecting. There was a leadership shakeup at the top of the company. I was given a job in the C suite. It was the first time I felt I actually had the power to make a difference and help the company get back on the right track. But the situation proved to be short-lived. The company was sold, there was yet another leadership shakeup, and the new CEO assembled a new leadership team. I was let go.

Thus ended my 15-year run in Corporate America.

If I hadn't been let go, how much longer would I have continued down that path? I honestly can't say for sure. But I hope that part of my story serves as a cautionary tale that helps someone avoid a prolonged period of ignoring what their heart is telling them.

I gave myself one day to feel frustration about the circumstances of pouring so much of myself into something, only to be booted out the door. And then I committed to turning the event into the positive catalyst I knew it could be.

In the days that followed my exit, I was suddenly afforded the distance and perspective I needed to make sense of the path I had been on so that I could learn and grow from it, and eventually help others in similar situations as well.

For starters, I mentioned before how it's been said that success at the wrong thing can lock you in forever. Be careful because it's true. My journey illustrates that point in spades. But now I can really see why. Success at something feels good. It feels good to be wanted and to be rewarded through promotions and such. Those are especially dangerous for someone like me who has had the tendency to place too much stock in external approval and financial security. Those two things don't satisfy in a deep way like purpose, meaning and serving others do, but they can be sticky without a doubt.

Another thing that became crystal clear to me is how careful you have to be about what jobs you say yes to, because it might be your job for a lot longer than you expect. We often tell ourselves, "I can always leave if it isn't working." But that's easier said than done for most people.

It may seem like I was just a total idiot for sticking it out on a path for as many years as I did. But the truth was I always only felt as though I was agreeing to stick it out in many of those roles for another three, six, or twelve months at most before I planned on leaving. I was waiting for a bonus, or I wanted to see a given project through, or I was overly hopeful the phase would pass and things would get better. But if you string enough of those three/six/twelve month periods together, a decade can pass in almost no time at all. Yikes.

And the longer you are with something, the more inertia you build up. I've said this before, but the more you have invested in something, the riskier it feels to be giving up what you've built for yourself by jumping ship. It's easy to end up stuck for a lot longer than you expected. And sometimes the discomfort has to become overwhelming before it's enough to overcome the inertia of staying the course.

So I hope you can also see why I caution continuing down a road you know is not right for you while you save up money. That, too, can lock you in for a lot longer than you expected.

Perhaps my most vital lesson from all of this was the absolute criticality of carving out time for self-reflection, self-discovery and listening for what you feel called to do on a deep level. As I look back, I see that the biggest force keeping me stuck throughout my 15-year corporate run was that I wasn't clear enough on what to do next. I kept assuming clarity would materialize on its own rather than taking proactive steps to coax it out from hiding using the approaches I suggested earlier in this book.

But it didn't... probably because I was too busy working incredibly hard at the wrong thing and never taking meaningful time to lift up my head and figure things out. So without knowing what I was aiming at, I wasn't able to take the next step forward. At each pivotal moment where I could have embraced the maxim of *always move closer*, I took the path of least resistance, often moving further away in the process.

The beautiful thing about being let go is that it gives you an unexpected amount of time on your hands. Thankfully, I had finally learned something and I knew better than to scramble and go get another job.

So I repurposed that time to finishing the job of self-reflection that I had made so much progress on during my 4 a.m. sessions. I took time to pursue some of the other recommendations I shared earlier in the book, including an incredibly clarifying week-long retreat.

I came away from the next several weeks with a sense of conviction that I wanted to make my life about helping people transform and grow through the practices that had been so powerful in my life, including mental training work like meditation, breathwork, and flow states, along with coaching, speaking, and leading workshops. I was also keen on seeing if I could help drive positive shifts in performance and well-being in the corporate environments I saw struggling so much.

As I contemplated how to bring all of this to life, the dusty yellow *Small Business for Dummies* book did its work on me without me ever having to open it. Its mere presence on my shelf for that number of years was a loud enough message that it couldn't be ignored. It was time to give it a shot and start my own business. Soon after this series of recognitions, my business was officially born. (If you're curious, you can find more about what I'm up to at mikekav.com.)

In the spirit of radical honesty, I have to admit that some of my desire to start a business stemmed from feeling jaded by my experiences working for other people and having my destiny be so subjected to the decision-making and misaligned values that characterized so much of my stint in Corporate America.

But moving away from something you wish to avoid is never as powerful as moving toward something you value. So my real source of motivation stems from moving toward an incredibly deep value of mine—pursuing the path that is truest to who I am with as few compromises as possible.

I know there are no guarantees in life. Inevitably, lots will change with the business. Things may not go according to plan. Is it possible I could fail and end up working for a corporation again? Sure, it's possible I could one day find myself tucking my tail between my legs and returning to that world as a matter of necessity. If that day ever comes, I hope I have the good sense to approach it in a dramatically different way than I did before. (For example, I would be insanely selective.) But that has to be my last resort. It's not that there aren't good companies out there that are honorable, rational and capable of providing people with a sense of purpose. It's simply that I have to see things *all the way through* on this path of pursuing a calling.

I have no idea how all of this will play out. That's for the universe to decide. But my focus is on doing my part, and I can say without a doubt that despite the uncertainty, the risk of failure and the challenges I have faced on my new path so far, I feel more whole and content than I ever have in my life.

There is one more promise I have made to myself on top of the other commitments I have articulated, and that is to live by the principles I have shared in this book—to make my pursuit of a calling my spiritual practice and to live a life I can be truly proud of that is free from regrets.

How is a person to judge his or success in something as subjective as living by a set of principles like these? For me, I do it through the lens of my children. Is my life a true model of the things I espouse?

So often, over the past couple of years, I have heard myself telling my son how important it is to "do what you love" in life. Every chance I get as my children grow up, I'll be telling them to follow their heart and I'll be warning them not to chase money, or prestige, or whatever else society dupes people into thinking makes us happy. I'll be telling them that contentment is about following their truth and being their authentic selves. Indeed, the advice we give to our kids is often advice we should be giving to ourselves.

But I know giving them advice is a weak substitute for showing them the fruits by actually *living it* myself. That is the essence of the commitment I am making to my children, to myself and to anyone who happens to read this.

I've already started by bringing my son into my process in this phase of my journey. I shared my ideas with him as I was in the self-reflection phase, and now I am sharing the progress I am making as I head down this new path in life.

Then, a couple of nights ago while lying in bed, we had this conversation:

Him: What did you do today?

Me: I went out for coffee with an old coworker. Then I came home and hung out with Mommy and Mrs. Bell, then I went and had coffee with another coworker before I came home, and then you came home from school.

Him: Sounds like your day was pretty boring.

Me: If you say so. It was fun to get to see people I hadn't seen in a while.

Him: So Daddy, how is your book going?

Me: Really well, I'm having a lot of fun writing it!

Him: How many pages is it?

Me: I'm not sure.

Him: What size font is it?

Me: I think it's 11.

Him: Are there pictures?

Me: No not at the moment, but there could be.

Him: Wait so how many years were you at your last job?

Me: Five.

Him: Wait so you were there five years... that means you were there when I was two years old. What job did you have when I was one?

Me: I worked at a consulting company. Consulting companies tell other companies what they should do to help try to fix them.

Him: Wait I didn't know you had other jobs! I only thought you worked at a bagel shop.

Me: Yeah that was my first job ever, when I was in high school. I just haven't told you about the other ones.

Him: So how much money did you make at the consulting place?

Me: Well I did consulting for a lot of years so I made more money toward the end versus when I started.

Him: And did you go up when you were at the bagel shop?

Me: No, I was only there a summer.

Him: How much did you make there?

Me: I think I made about six dollars an hour. I usually worked about six hours a day.

Him: So 36 dollars a day. Hmm that's pretty good. What other jobs did you have?

Me: I also worked in a tennis club for a summer, in a research lab in grad school, and I taught high school and middle school for a little while.

Him: You worked in a lab?

Me: Yeah. I looked in microscopes.

Him: How much money did you make?

Me: I probably made two thousand dollars for the summer.

Him: That's pretty good.

Me: Yeah, I guess it was. It helped me pay for my rent. It also taught me stuff that helped me get into grad school.

Him: So what is the lowest amount you ever made?

Me: The tennis club paid me minimum wage which was about five dollars an hour. Minimum wage is the lowest a company is allowed to pay by law.

Him: What's the highest somebody can make?

Me: There's no limit. Like someone who owns a really big company could make lots of money.

Him: So how many pages is your book again?

Me: I'm not sure.

Him: Just guess.

Me: Maybe seventy so far.

Him: Are you writing about the bagel shop?

Me: No, I wasn't going to write about the bagel shop. The earliest job I talked about was when I was in my twenties.

Him: You should write about the bagel shop.

Me: Really?

Him: Yes definitely.

Me: Okay, I guess I could do that.

Him: Just delete where it says "Once upon a time..." No actually, just make some space after where it says "Once upon a time..." and then put it there.

Me: Ah, after 'Once upon a time.' Okay, will do.

Him: Daddy, we started this conversation talking about what you did today and now we're talking about this. That's so cool how conversations do that.

Me: Yeah that is one of the fun things about conversations, isn't it?

Him: Goodnight Daddy. I love you.

Me: Goodnight. I love you too.

PART 4:

Your Success Story

Is there anything holding you back?

We've come a long way. If you have reached this point, that's a strong message that there is something within you that is pulled toward pursuing a livelihood of purpose, meaning and passion.

Is there anything still holding you back?

If your answer to that is a definitive "no" and you're ready to charge forward, then do it!

But for anyone who wants to be on the path of pursuing a calling but is still feeling hesitant or stuck, let's see if we can root out those last vestiges of resistance. Those feelings can come up further down the path as well, so learning to spot them can help prevent them from grinding you to a halt if they do arise.

If you find yourself wavering, it's time to exercise your self-awareness muscle again and get to the root of *why* you are feeling hesitant or stuck. Keep in mind that the surface-level reason for why you are feeling the way you are feeling isn't always the full story. Often there is an even deeper *why* underneath it. Becoming aware of the true reason behind your hesitancy is the most important lever for releasing it.

Let's take a look at a few of the most common sources of these feelings.

Fear of failure

If there is one feeling that is the most ubiquitous culprit in preventing people from going for it in life, it is the fear of failure.

I get it. It's daunting to consider the possibility that things could go wrong. And human beings are hardwired to avoid fear. It takes conscious effort and courage to move through fear.

When fear gets the better of us, one effective way to approach it is to get closer to it. Instead of resisting the fear (or fearing the fear), which only adds to how real it feels, go in the other direction. Give into the fear completely and let it run wild by imagining the absolute worst case scenario unfolding.

It's helpful to write this one in your journal. Take some time to think about every possible way things could go wrong. Give yourself entirely to the thought experiment. Be as thorough and vivid as possible as you bring the worst case scenario to life in your imagination and get it down on paper.

Once you've done that, take a look at what your imagination has conjured up and reflect on it. Now that it's all out there in the worst form you could imagine, how bad is it really? Could you survive through the ugliest worst case scenario?

And how likely is it that all of that would come true? What do you think would actually end up happening if things didn't go so well?

When we give ourselves to this reflection, usually what we find is that the things we fear most about taking the leap of faith are overblown in our minds. Because we weren't looking directly at the fearful thoughts and exposing them for what they were, they had power over us. They were like an animal puffing itself up to make itself look larger and more menacing than it really is, as if to say "Please take me seriously." As soon as we look directly at the things we fear, we often see that they aren't as bad as we thought and that the realistic downsides we may experience are likely to be much milder than the fears would have us believe.

One major source of fear we tend to have has to do with a threat to our financial security. But far from the fear that tells us "I [or we] will end up going hungry and living on the streets," we see that no matter how things turn out, we will be okay. Plenty of people have experienced incredible financial hardship—often much more severe than we are likely to face—and those people have lived through it. In many cases, they found something beneficial that came from the experience, such as discovering a resilience they never knew they had. And lots of people have lost everything only to rebuild themselves. This is not to downplay the potential difficulties, it's simply to put them into perspective.

Another common fear we have is: *If I fail, what will other people think?* We are afraid of what failure would do to our self-image and our sense of self-worth.

The more we mature, the less this fear tends to have a hold on us. We go beyond living through the lens of other people because we see that it is an inherently unsatisfying way to live.

But even if other people's opinions are of genuine concern, here is the surprising thing that usually happens if a person goes for it and ends up failing. (I know this because many of the people I have talked with have shared this with me about the failures they have experienced.) Contrary to their expectation that people would think less of them, most people thought *more* of them. People would share sentiments with them like, "Good for you for being willing to take a risk. Not many people would do that."

Failure is hard. And there are no guarantees things will work out the way you hope, so failure is a real possibility.

But as hard as failure can be, it's never the end of the road. It is a defining moment, without a doubt. But it always has the potential to make us wiser, stronger and more resilient. And once we have experienced failure and we have seen that it wasn't as bad as we expected, we become that much more fearless.

I also encourage you to never forget this:

As risky as the potential for failure seems, it's rarely as risky as playing it safe and inviting regrets into your life. You only have this one life. You have the power to make yours an amazing life by choosing to set sail and taking the journey. You can overcome a failure and still live an incredible life. But how incredible can your life be if you spend it clinging to the shore?

Fear of success

Let's take a look at another source of inner resistance. This one can be more difficult to identify because it seems to run counter to logic.

It is the fear of success.

The *fear of success* sounds paradoxical to many people. *Why would I be afraid to succeed?*

The reason the fear of success exists is because succeeding means we have to let go of the old paradigm on some level. As much as we may think we want to move on from the way things are and move toward our aspirational vision, there is often a part of us that is afraid to let go of the old and embrace the new.

This is the same phenomenon that keeps us holding onto things that are distinctly negative in life, such as a familiar source of discomfort or pain. Perhaps you've witnessed this with someone you know, or maybe you've experienced it in your own life. The decision to stay in a bad relationship is a prime example of this phenomenon at work. As clear as it may be that the relationship doesn't serve our highest good, we may find it extraordinarily difficult to let the relationship go.

Very few people are immune to this phenomenon. There are lots of potential behaviors and decisions across many realms of our lives that we may find ourselves continuing to pursue despite our knowing that our choices aren't in our best interest. Usually we continue because our behaviors and decisions are familiar and bring us some sense of comfort.

If we have trouble letting go of things that we know are negative on the whole, imagine how difficult it can be to let go of things we value.

One of the most common examples of this on the path of pursuing a calling is the situation where our decisions don't have the approval or support of loved ones. Any time our path doesn't conform to other people's desires and expectations, we're faced with a choice—do we honor ourselves or do we hold onto our need to please those around us?

One way the fear of success can manifest in this situation is that we start to feel wobbly about our decision to move forward. We think our feelings of reservation are the result of other fears like being afraid to fail. But in actuality, our minds are playing a trick on us. Our deeper fear has to do with a concern about growing apart from friends or family, or not having the love and support of people who are close to us.

This self-deception is the reason the fear of success can be difficult to identify. It can present itself as something other than itself without us being aware of it.

One sign that fear of success may be at play in your life is if you notice any patterns indicative of self-sabotage. This could be the feeling that you don't deserve things to work out according to your highest aspirations, or it could be a feeling of unworthiness, or it could be feelings of guilt about your success. Self-sabotage may show up in ways that are more hidden, such as the recurring tendency for things to fall apart for you just when they start to get good.

You deserve to succeed. You are worthy of an amazing life. Yes, you may have to go against the grain. It's not always possible to please everyone in life. But it's so much more important to honor the call of your heart than to conform to the expectations others place on you. Other people may eventually come around and accept your new direction in life, but it's hard to overcome a betrayal of your own heart. Stay true to that which you know is right for you.

Too many possibilities

Sometimes we find ourselves hesitating to move forward because we aren't sure which way to go in light of all of the possibilities. So instead we just stay put.

A common time for this to happen is right after graduating school. Recent graduates may feel lost simply because they are too early in their journey to know which way to proceed. The world offers so many possibilities, and although many of them may be viable and satisfying paths, it is difficult to decide in the absence of more life experience.

This problem of too many possibilities can also stall the individual who has too many passions, but usually for a different reason. A person with too many passions often has trouble with the idea of picking a direction because it means they have to narrow their focus and let go of some of the other things they love.

If you find yourself in the former group and are having trouble picking a direction because you are early in your journey, I encourage you to open yourself to the prospect of a little trial and error. Do your best to orient yourself in the direction of something that tugs at your heart and then take the plunge.

As hard as it may be to accept the possibility that you may end up heading in a so-called wrong direction, it's not important to get it perfectly right on your first attempt. It's more important to learn how to rapidly adapt based on what you uncover through experience. The truth is that it's almost impossible to "get it perfectly right" anyway. Even if you enjoy what you do, chances are you'll want to try other things out. Your tastes may change. You may feel pulled in other directions.

But if you focus on remaining flexible and agile, then you're able to hone in on the right direction much more quickly. You're also able to rapidly recover from any potential missteps. In retrospect, if I could have learned any superpower earlier on in my journey, I would have chosen it to be this one. This would have saved me a ton of time and energy and mitigated a tremendous amount of the headaches I experienced on my path.

If you find yourself in the latter group of people whose hesitancy stems from having too many interests that are difficult to choose between, remember that your decision to head in a direction does not mean that you are closing the door to the other opportunities forever.

Yes, there are only so many things a person can take on at one time. It's important not to spread yourself too thin, or you may end up digging too many wells that are only one-foot deep.

But instead of viewing the decision to narrow your focus as a letting go or sacrifice of some of your passions, consider saving some of your passions for the next chapter in your life. Lots of people shift the focus of their livelihood multiple times over the course of their lives. There is plenty of time to pursue multiple passions if you take this approach.

Don't let yourself become paralyzed by too many options. Nothing is permanent. You have the power to adjust course along the way if you focus on remaining flexible and agile. Trust in your heart's ability to point you in a good direction and take the leap of faith.

Times are too uncertain

What do we do if we feel ready to pursue a calling but the external circumstances we find ourselves in do not seem conducive to our success?

This is a common sentiment during tough economic periods like recessions. Amidst an economic trough, many people are unemployed and it's easy to feel like we're lucky to have any job at all, even if it's not the job we truly want to be doing. Oftentimes employers capitalize on this feeling as well. They may cut back on people's pay or they may allow the quality of working conditions to decline because they know people are less likely to jump ship.

During a period like this, it can feel harder to make a move. The job market isn't as robust. It's a tougher time to make a business succeed because it's harder to secure loans and because potential customers are pulling back and spending less of their money on goods and services.

It's natural for external conditions like these to color our perspective. If anyone needs to hang onto a job or to take a job they would rather not take out of financial necessity, this is understandable. You have to do what you have to do.

213

But it's also true that plenty of people find jobs during recessions. There are always employers in search of good talent. And many successful businesses have opened their doors for the first time during economic downturns.

The most important thing is to be honest with ourselves about any decision we make. Sometimes we choose a less desirable path out of necessity, but other times we just convince ourselves it's a necessity when it's really just the reptilian part of our brain looking for any excuse to take the safe road. There is nothing wrong with playing it safe for a time if that's what feels right to you. But don't allow yourself to get stuck on the wrong path. Stay committed to your aspirations.

Freedom

It has been said that the mind is a wonderful servant but a horrible master. If we channel its energies into what it does best, it can be an effective problem-solver that helps us chart our course from where we are to where we want to be. But left unchecked, the mind can churn out fears and inner resistance that block us from pursuing the path that leads to our deepest sense of freedom and contentment.

Whenever we are confronted by fears and insecurities that are holding us back, our main job is to see them and to understand them. This seeing helps free us from the hold they have on us. We don't have to get rid of them. The freedom comes from recognizing that what they say isn't the absolute truth of the matter. When we see that the stories that the fears and insecurities are telling us are one perspective, and usually a limited one at that, then we are free to choose to move forward in spite of them. The more repetition and practice we have with moving forward in the face of our fears, the more we become comfortable with discomfort. And the greater our ability to push through discomfort, the more we open ourselves to the most magnificent rewards on this path.

It's a marathon,
not a sprint

Pursuing a calling is one of the highest paths a person can trek in life. It challenges us. It stretches us. It breaks us down only to build us up in new and transformed ways.

We're all aware of the archetypal images of the people who lose themselves in their meaningful work because it's such a part of who they are. We've seen the entrepreneurs working 16-hour days every day of the week to stand up their creation. We've seen the researchers who dedicate their every waking hour to the next discovery. We've seen the self-sacrifice of doctors who commit themselves day and night to helping keep others alive. Indeed, it can be quite beautiful to watch someone do amazing things through their passion and commitment to their cause.

But I want you to be in this for the long haul. And that means remembering that the path of pursuing a livelihood of purpose is a marathon, not a sprint.

Marathoners pace themselves. They hydrate and refuel along the way. If they go through a tough stretch like a long hill, they may pull back for a short time so they don't run out of gas.

When you're on the path of pursuing a calling, similar principles apply. Set a pace that you can handle over the long-term without burning yourself out. If you do go through a stretch that requires a disproportionate amount of hustle such as the early days of standing up a new endeavor, it's important to carve out time to pull back and recharge. You need to stay "hydrated" through self-care regimens. Balance is crucial.

I'm a big advocate for building daily rituals that include the kinds of practices that refuel you and keep your energy levels high. Make time for exercise. Eat healthy foods. Carve out time for yourself to recover, relax and recharge. Find practices that help keep you balanced, such as meditation, walks in nature, or whatever suits you.

Likewise, pay attention to when things get out of balance. If your livelihood starts consuming too much of you at the expense of other important aspects of your life, it's critical to recognize when that is happening and to be proactive about rebalancing things. If important relationships are starving, take the time to prioritize them. If your physical or mental health show any signs of wear, carve out space to cultivate good health. Avoid making extraordinary sacrifices that you may regret down the line.

This not only prevents potential regrets from becoming a reality, but it also positions you for long-term success because your path is sustainable.

I know it isn't always easy to juggle the different aspects of our lives that compete for our time and energy. We may feel a bit like someone spinning plates on sticks. As soon as we get one spinning again, another one is wobbly. We run over and spin that one, and then a new one is wobbly.

There's no question that we all have limited time and we have to make tradeoffs. But what I have found is that those who maintain a sustainable pace and prioritize healthy balance tend to do better in the long run. Even though it may appear as though they are limiting their potential gains in an endeavor by doing this, in the end they have staying power, they have higher energy levels, and most importantly, they are more fulfilled.

There is a straightforward reason for this. It's because the joy of pursuing a calling does not come from reaching a particular outcome. This is where the marathon analogy breaks down. There isn't some finish line we are striving toward. Any time we fall into the trap of thinking, "If I can just get to that point…" we soon find that we've reached that point only to discover that we have replaced it with a new arbitrary finish line. When I see people sprinting as hard as they can toward some point in the future, I think to myself, "Where do you think you are going?" There is no magic point we will reach in the future where we feel, "I've finally arrived."

The joy of pursuing a calling comes from our enjoyment of the process. It comes from our love of the journey itself. It really is about discovering satisfaction each step along the way. Even the difficult points become a part of a much bigger picture that fulfills us on a deeper level.

Do what you love. Love what you do. Love it not because of where it leads, but because of the enjoyment it brings you here and now.

Your success story

Imagine you wake up each morning and genuinely look forward to what you're going to be doing that day. Far from it feeling like a slog, the work you are about to do is something you truly enjoy.

As the day progresses, you hardly notice the time going by. You're focused and attentive. You feel creative and energized. By the time you stop to take a break, hours have passed. You're satisfied with your sense of progress.

After some more time working, you reach a stopping point for the day. You could certainly keep going; you still have plenty of energy to continue. But you have other priorities to tend to, so you decide that this is as good a time as any to shift gears. You feel really good about what you've accomplished that day and move onto the next part of your day feeling satisfied and energized.

For the rest of your day, you enjoy your time wholeheartedly. You feel present. You feel like the best version of yourself.

When it comes time to get back to your livelihood again, there's no sense of disappointment or dread. There's no clinging to your free time, wishing you didn't have to get back to work. There's no pervasive feeling of overwhelm, worry or stress. There's no "I need another vacation," or "I wish could retire and never have to work another day of my life."

That's not to imply that you never encounter challenges, that you never experience stress, or that every day is a day at the beach. But on the whole, your days are really good. You learn, you grow, you exercise your creativity, and you have a sense of autonomy. You are great at what you do. Your work feels important. When you take a step back, you feel like you are making a real difference. When you reach important milestones with respect to your livelihood, they bring you a deep sense of pride and satisfaction. And when you zoom out and look at your life, you feel happy and fulfilled, like you wouldn't want to be anywhere else other than where you are right now.

Is all of this a pipe dream? I don't think so.

To me, this is what is available to us when we choose to commit ourselves to the journey of doing what we love. It's available to us if we are willing to take the risk and follow the road less traveled.

Take time to visualize your own success story—your unique version of a life of true contentment. If you are willing to turn this into a daily practice, even better. Do it even if you're in the midst of your journey. Imagine in full detail what your life looks like when you give yourself completely to this path and your life becomes a reflection of your highest aspirations. What are you doing? Who are you doing it alongside? Where are you? What is the environment you find yourself in? What does your typical day look like? What are some of the big milestones and accomplishments you reach?

What is it about your new life that brings you the most satisfaction and joy?

As you visualize this for yourself with as much specificity as possible, imagine it has become a reality and really *feel* what it feels like to have all of this come true for yourself. Suspend any speck of disbelief and pour yourself completely into it. Step into the feeling state. Convince your physical and emotional body it has come true. There is incredible power in doing this. It is one of the most effective ways to shed the limitations that exist in your own mind. It is one of the most potent ways to instill in yourself the belief that all of this is possible.

Because it *is* possible.

We know it's possible because we have seen such things come true for lots of other people.

So why not you? You aren't fundamentally different from any of those people. Honestly, why can't it be you?

Deep in your heart you know what you feel called to do. You know how good your life can be. You just need to go for it. Be open and flexible, of course, and allow yourself multiple paths on the journey. But do whatever it takes to stay the course. Follow the light within yourself that leads you to where your highest self knows you should be headed. And be a light for the rest of us. Your story can pave the way for so many others to follow.

Stay true to this, and the rest is basically magic.

I wish you nothing but the best on your incredible journey.

Acknowledgments

I received so much support during the years I was working on this book. I owe a deep debt of gratitude to Jon Allegretto, Jen Bachelder, Alison Hardy, Ross Dettman, Damon and Edward Daniels. Without their generosity, this book would not have been possible. But on a deeper level, my own journey would not have unfolded the way it did had it not been for each of them sharing their time, their stories and their hard-earned lessons with me.

My sincere thanks go to Dan Murphy for his assistance in honing the manuscript and helping me push it over the finish line.

I am also thankful for the tremendous support of Christina Moritz. Without her continued encouragement and active contributions from the earliest stage of this project to today, this book and my journey of pursuing a calling never would have come to fruition the way it did.

And finally, I owe heartfelt thanks to my family for the love and support they have given me throughout this phase of personal transformation and growth, and especially to Brody for his help in bringing this book to life.

About the Author

Mike Kavanagh began work on *What Is Your Calling? The Journey to Find Work You Love* when he was asking himself that very question. Although he had experienced success working in senior roles in corporations, he felt drawn to finding work that was capable of fulfilling him on a deeper level. His multi-year journey of self-discovery dovetailed with the writing of this book, making it a uniquely authentic and valuable resource for people in the midst of their own process of finding and pursuing their true calling.

Kavanagh recently set out to build a livelihood around his calling. He is the author of two other books:

Coach's Plan: The Personal Productivity System That Changed My Life

The Successful Manager: Practical Approaches for Building and Leading High-Performing Teams

You can find out more about his work, as well as his free content, at mikekav.com.